I0502605

Amazing Mandalas Coloring Book

Copyright: Published in the United States by James Hinson
Published December 2016
ISBN-13: 978-1541298903
ISBN-10: 154129890X

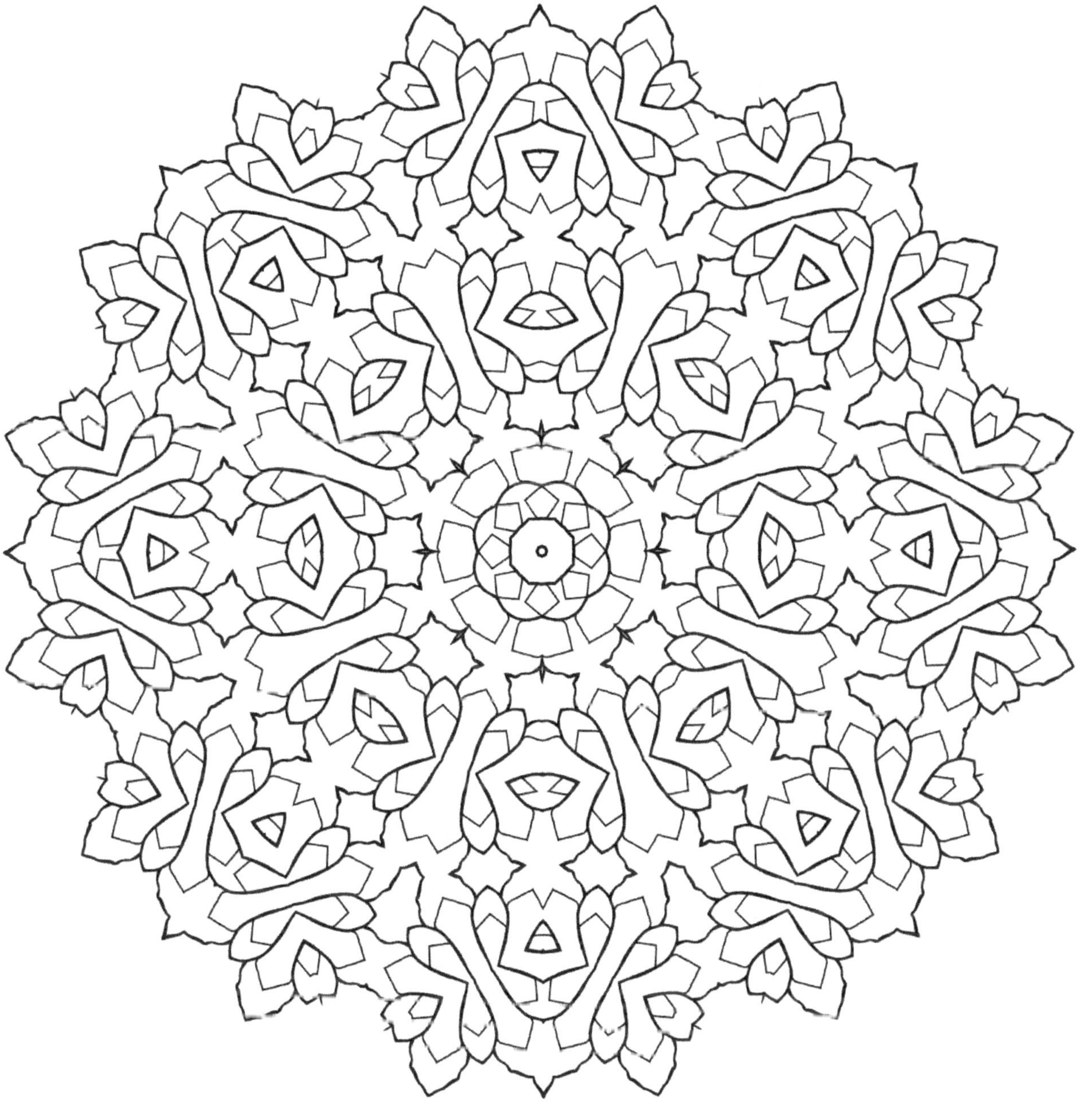

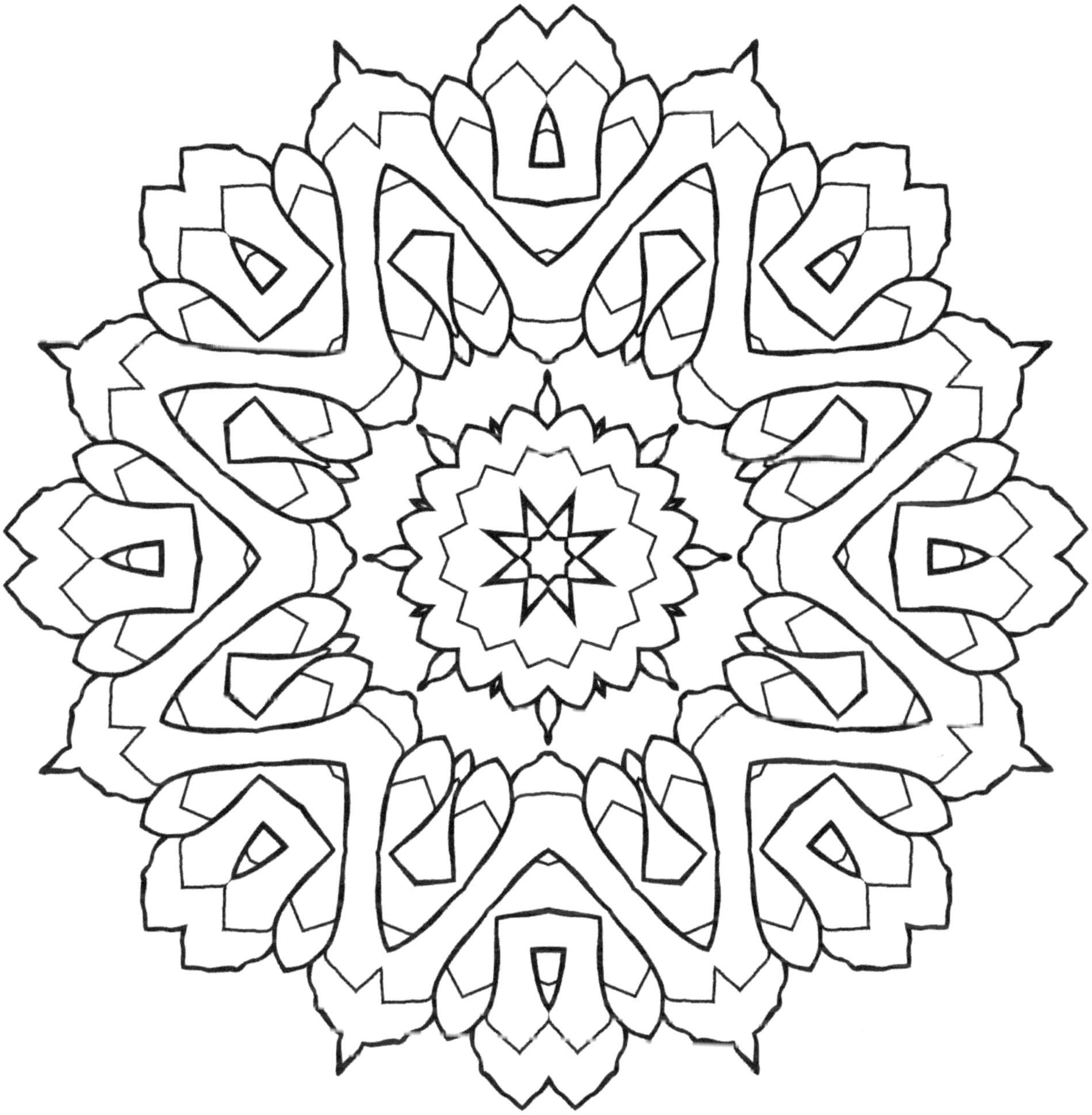

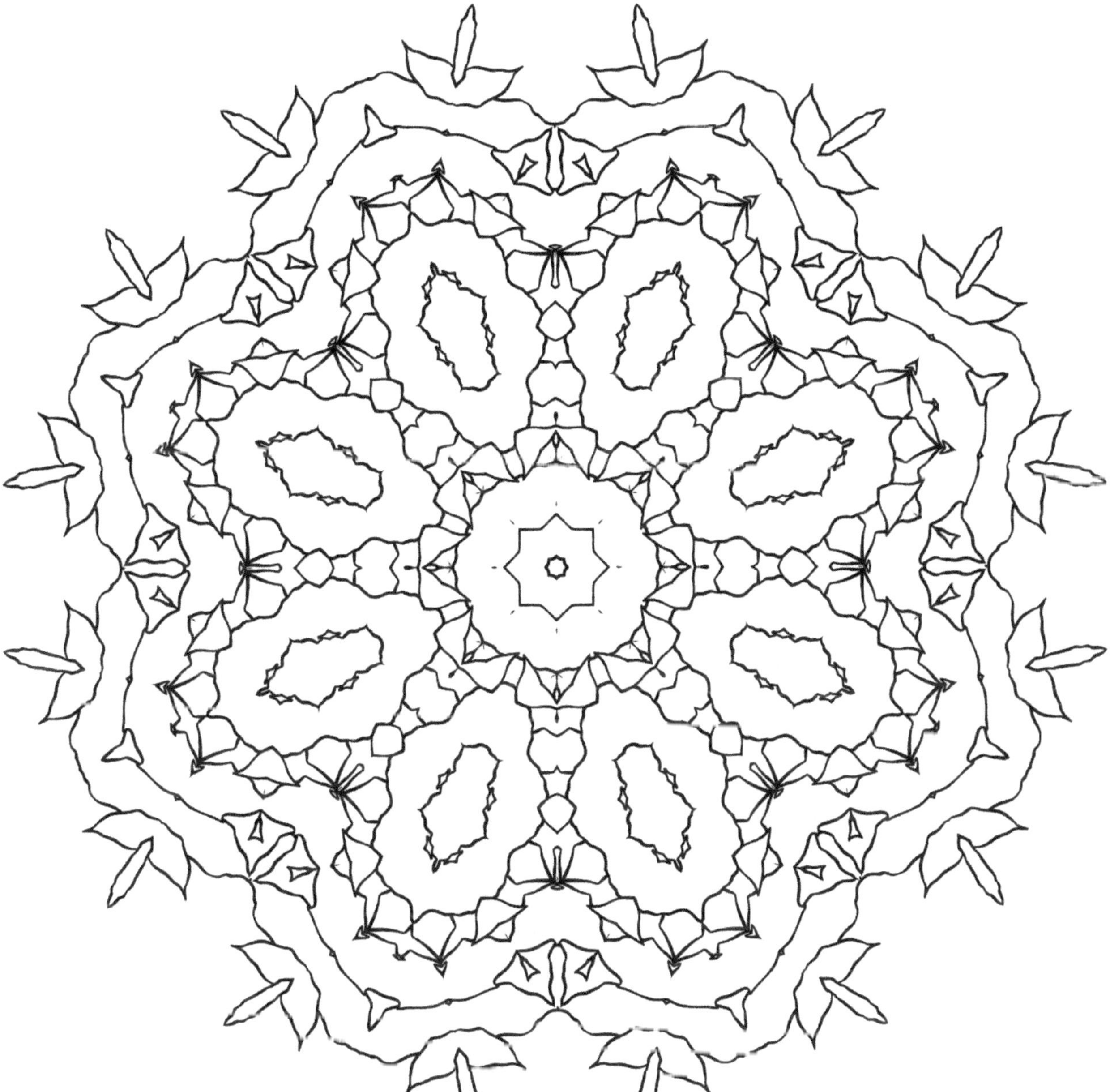

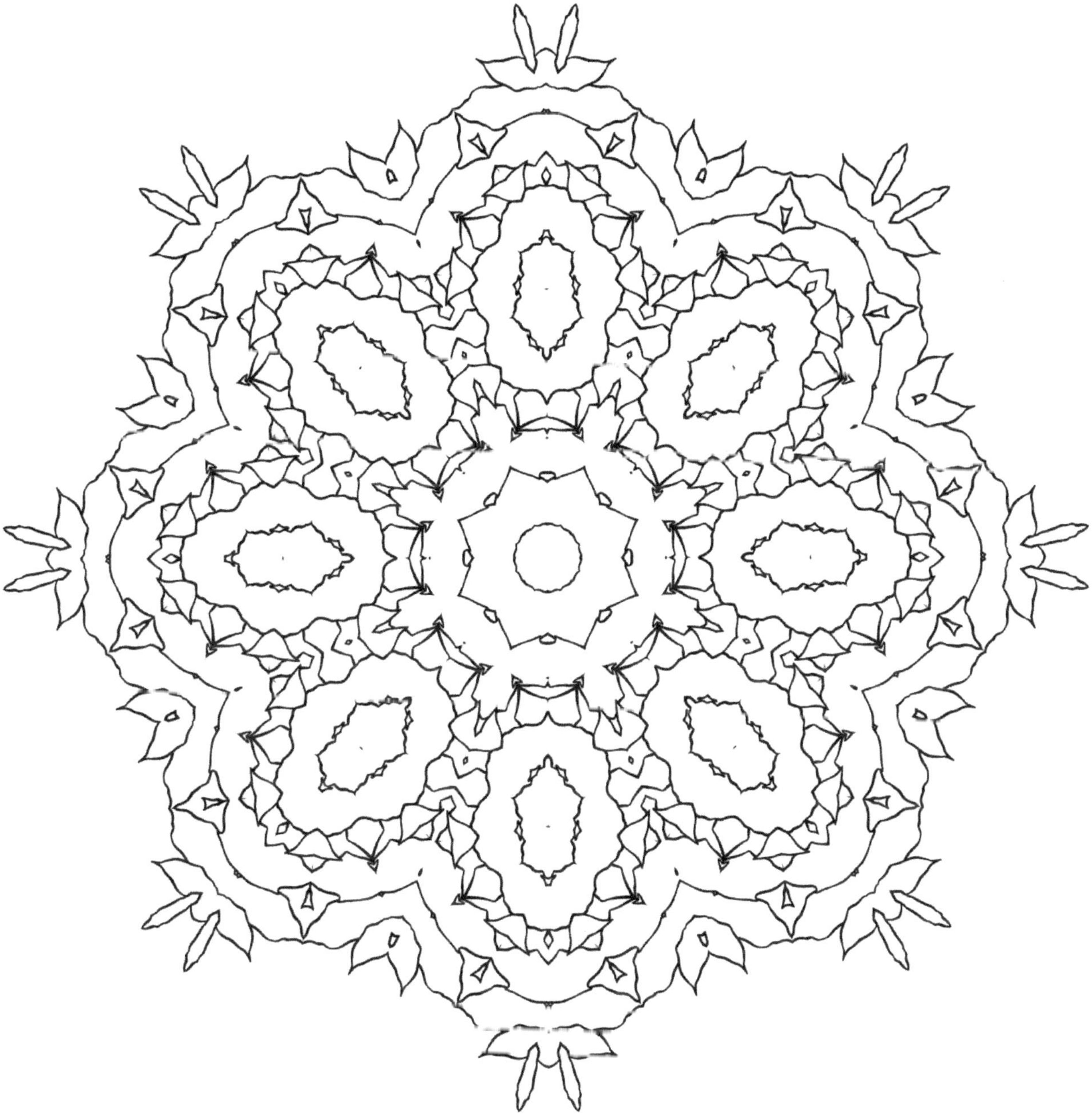

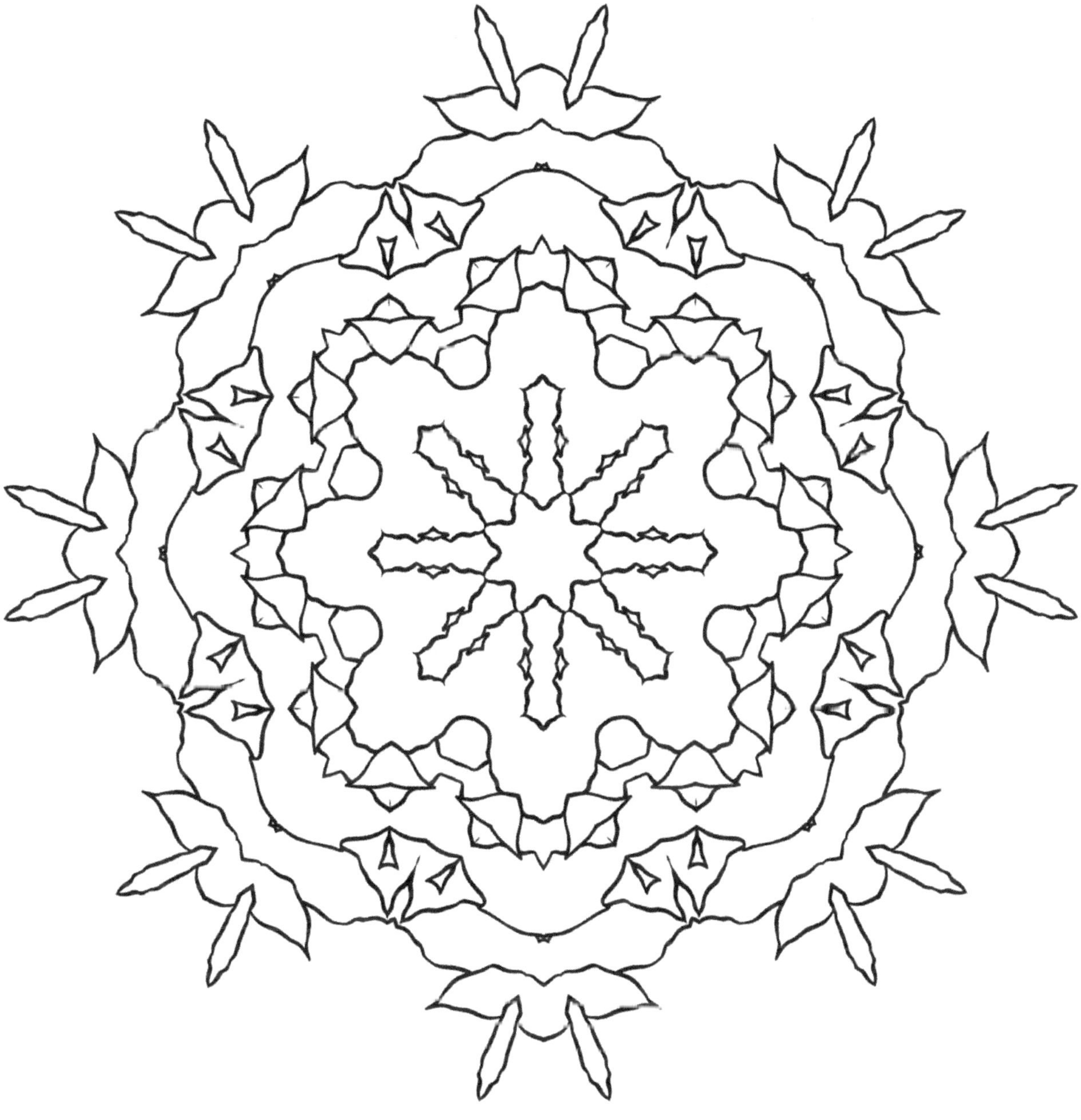

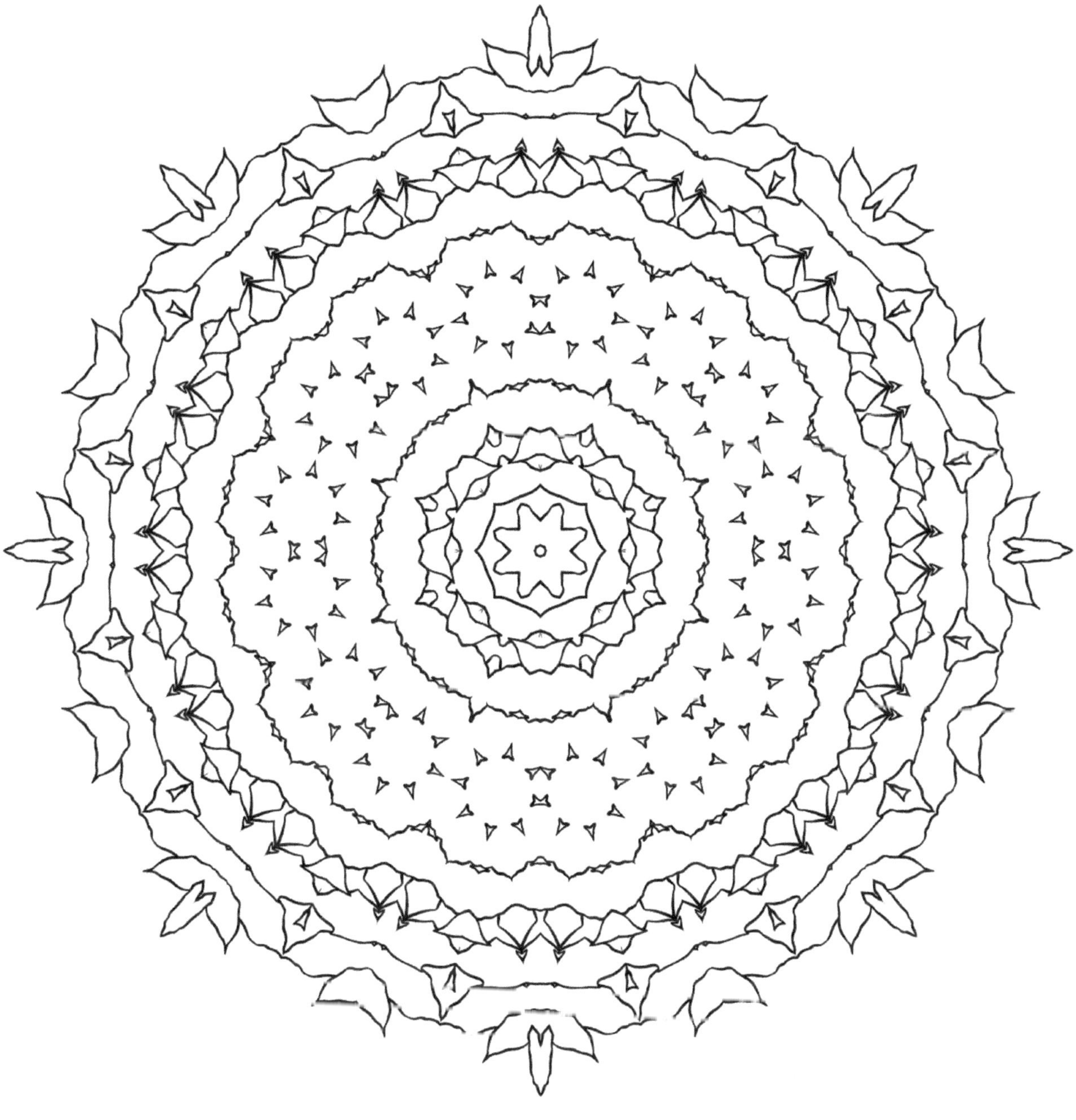

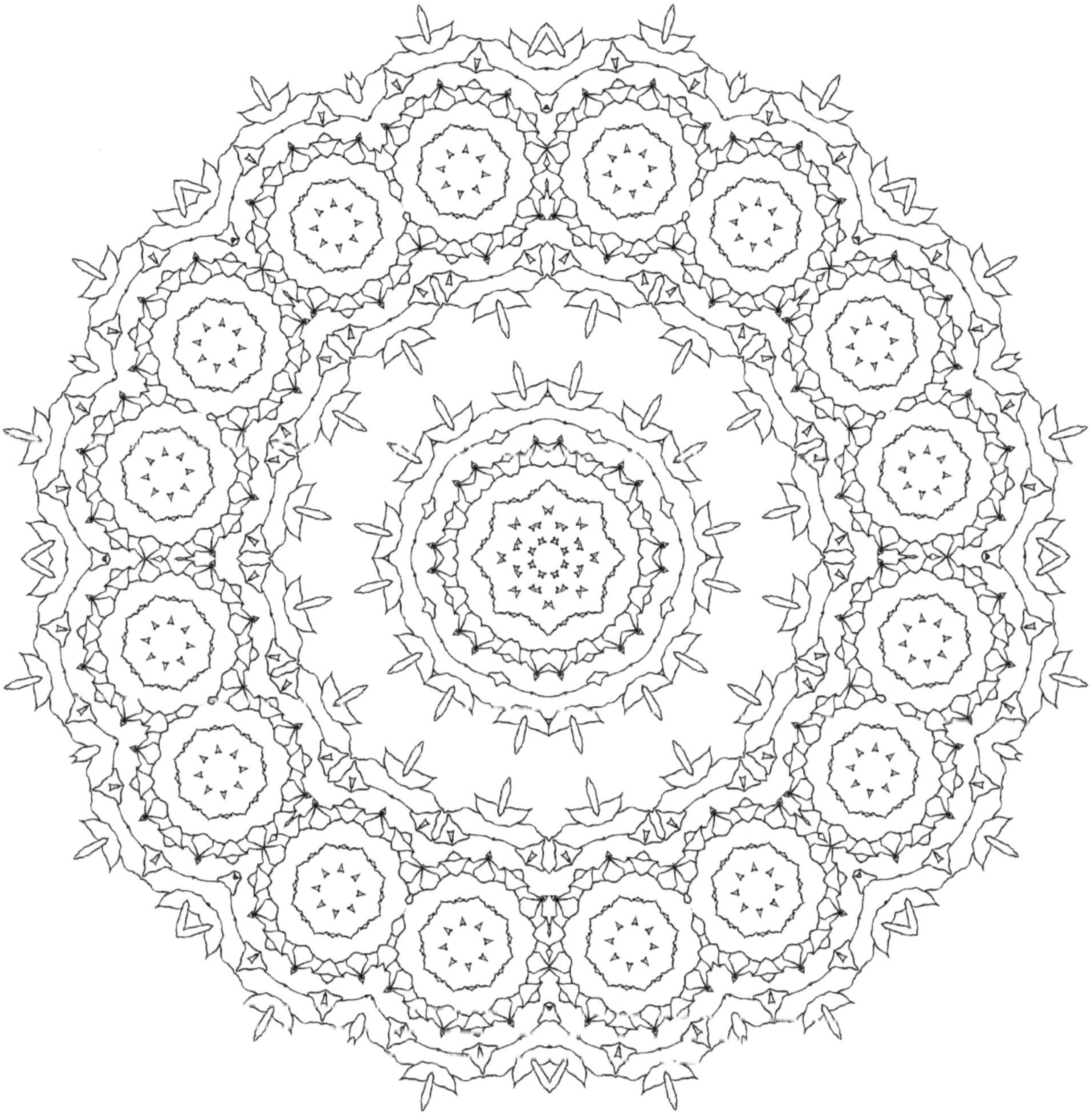

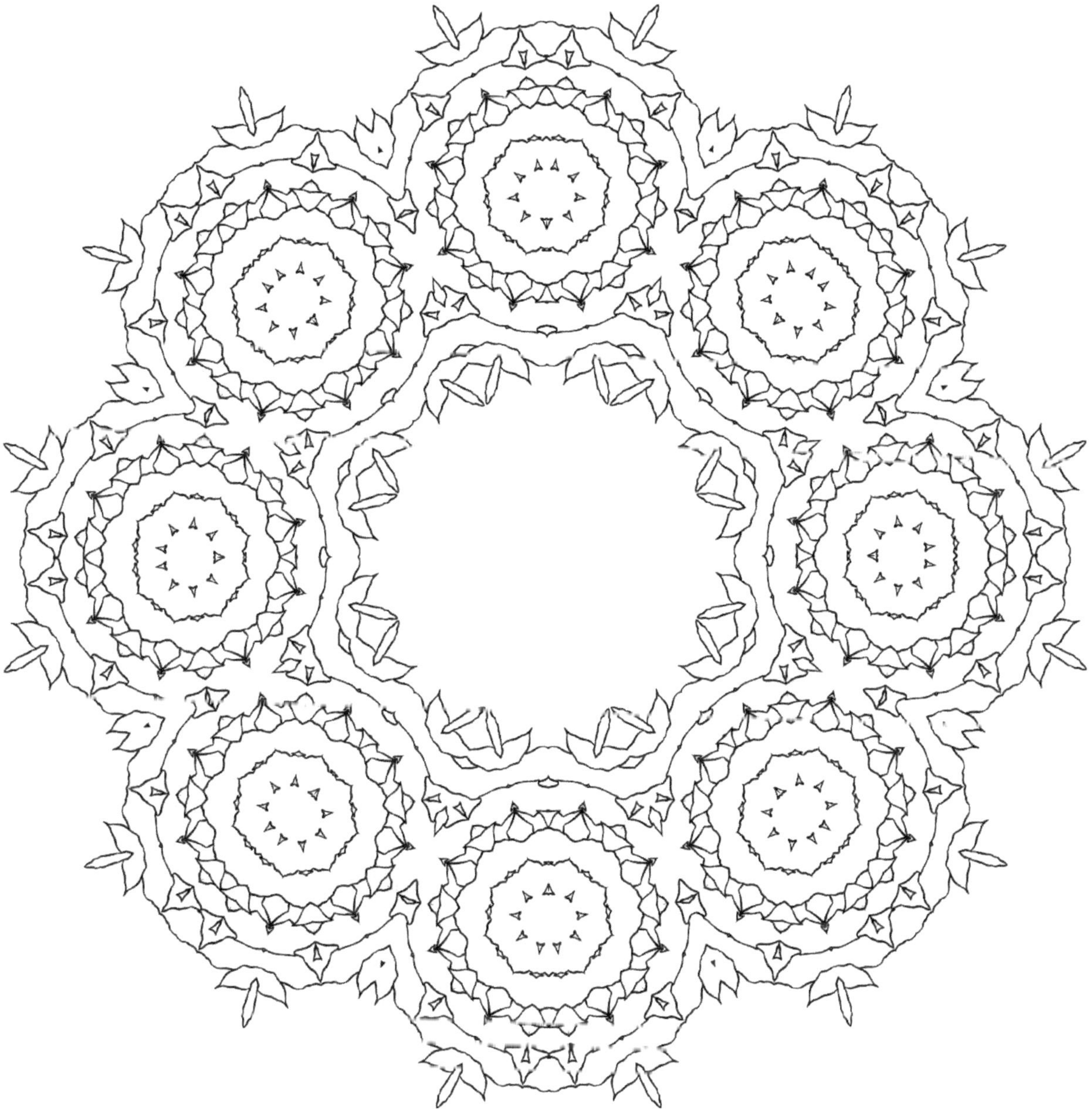

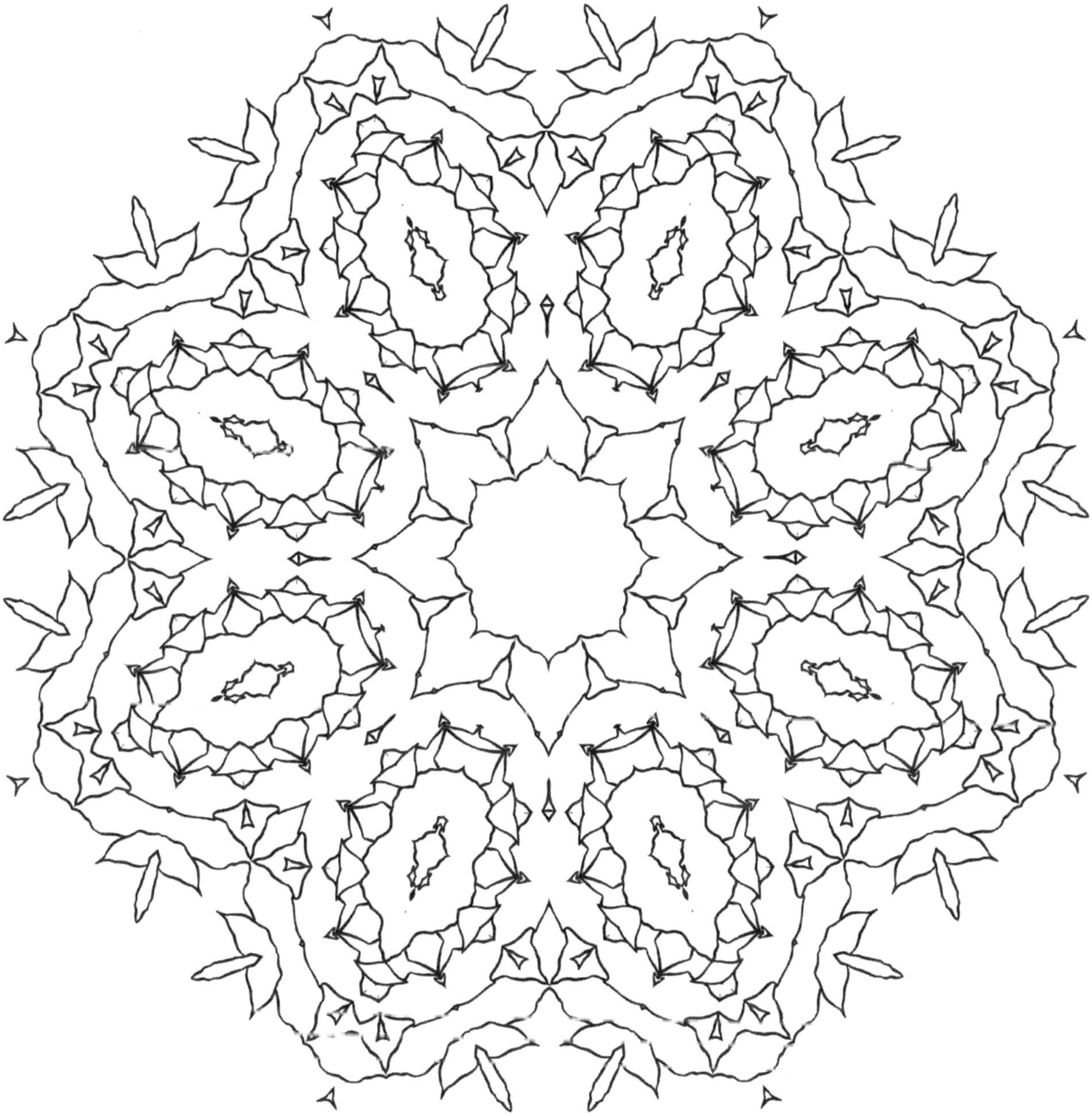

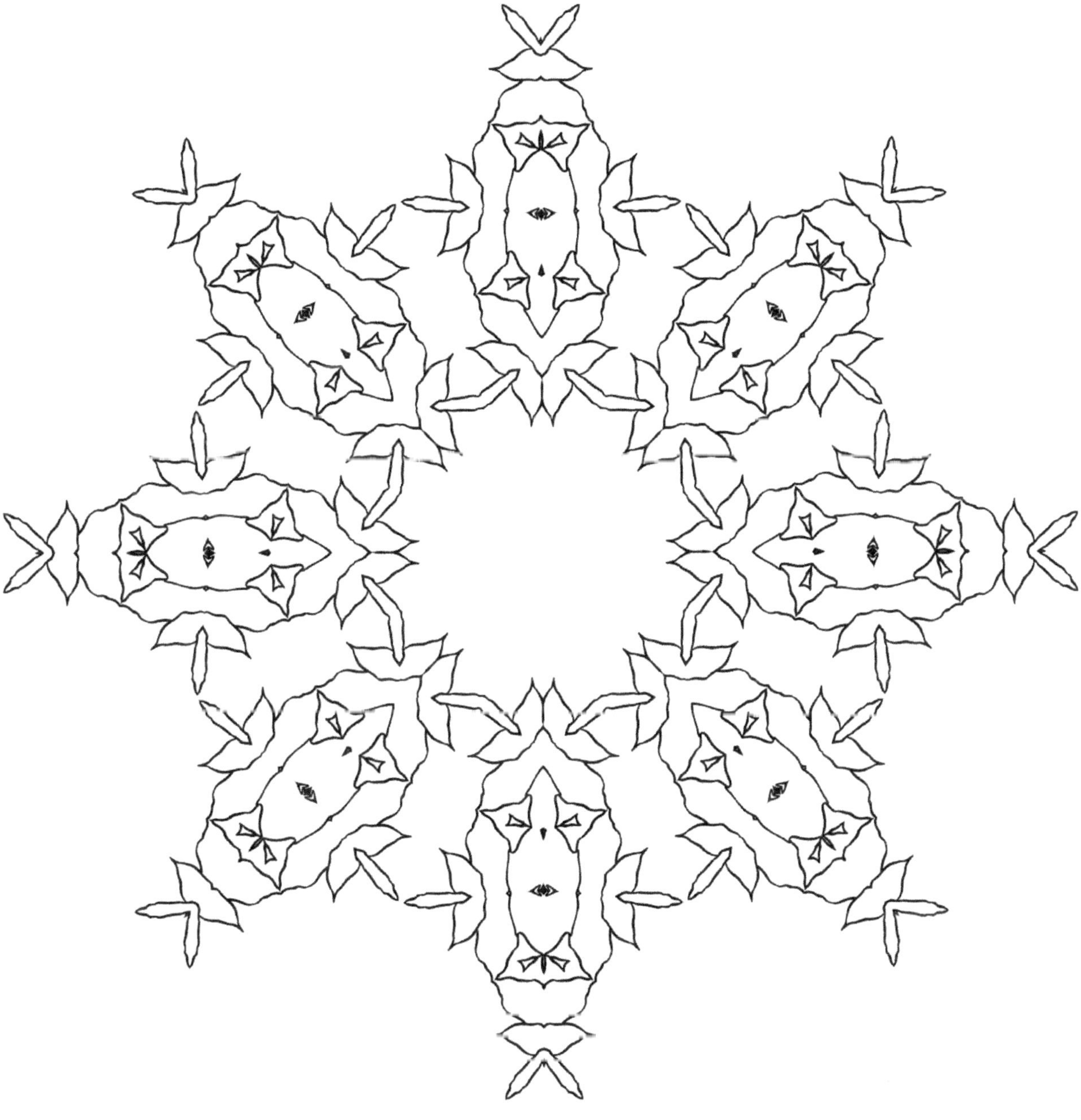

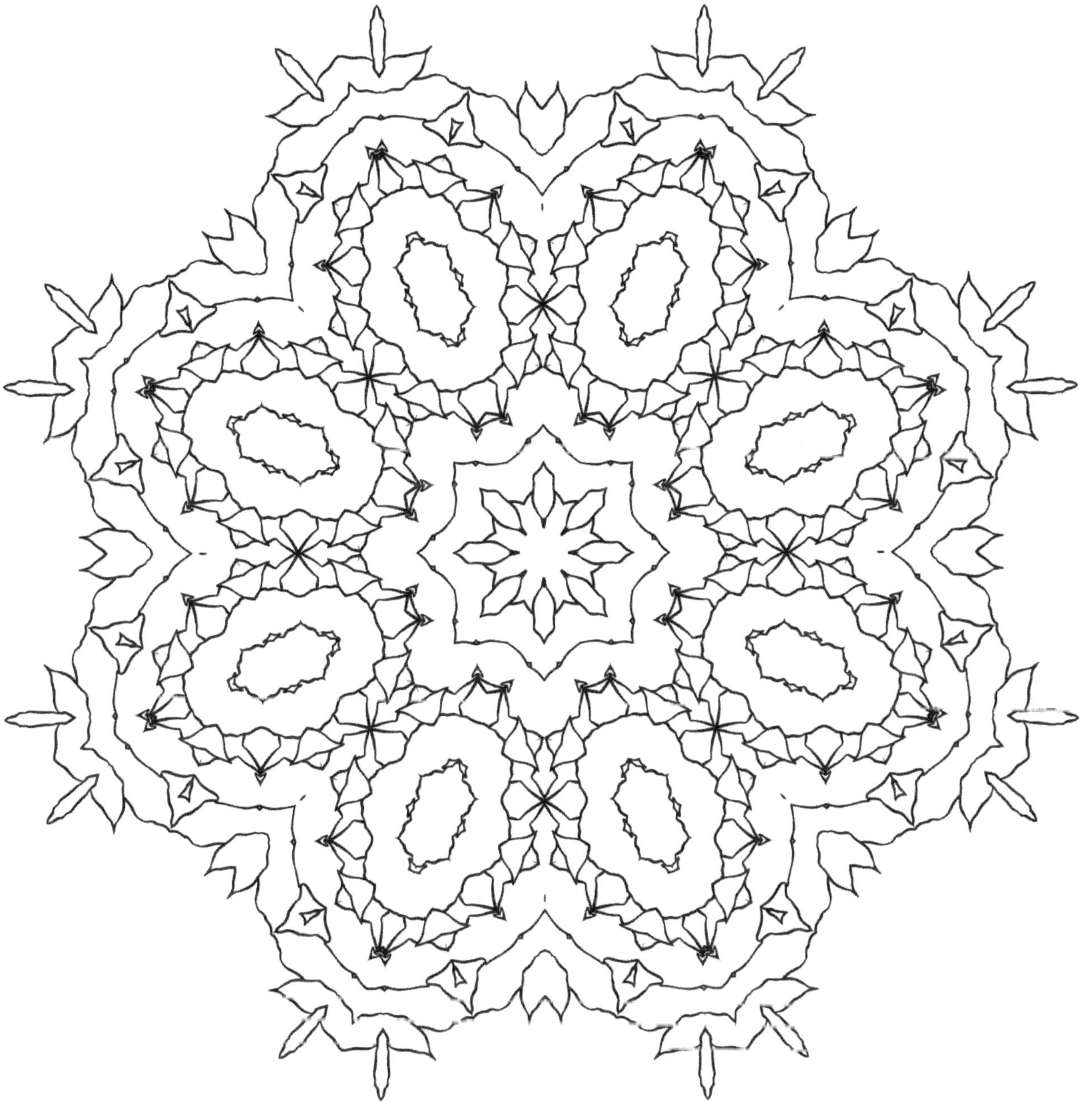

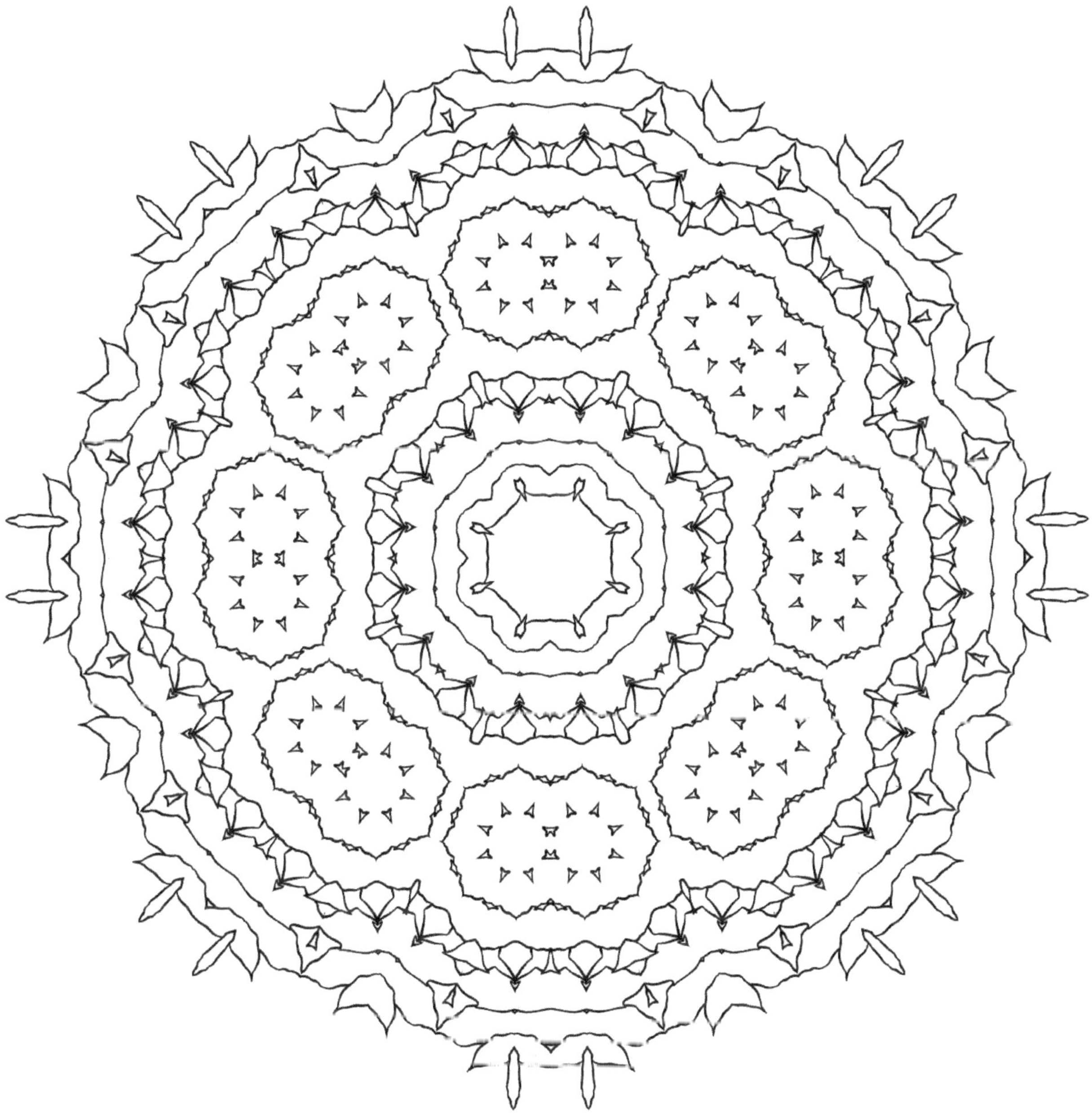

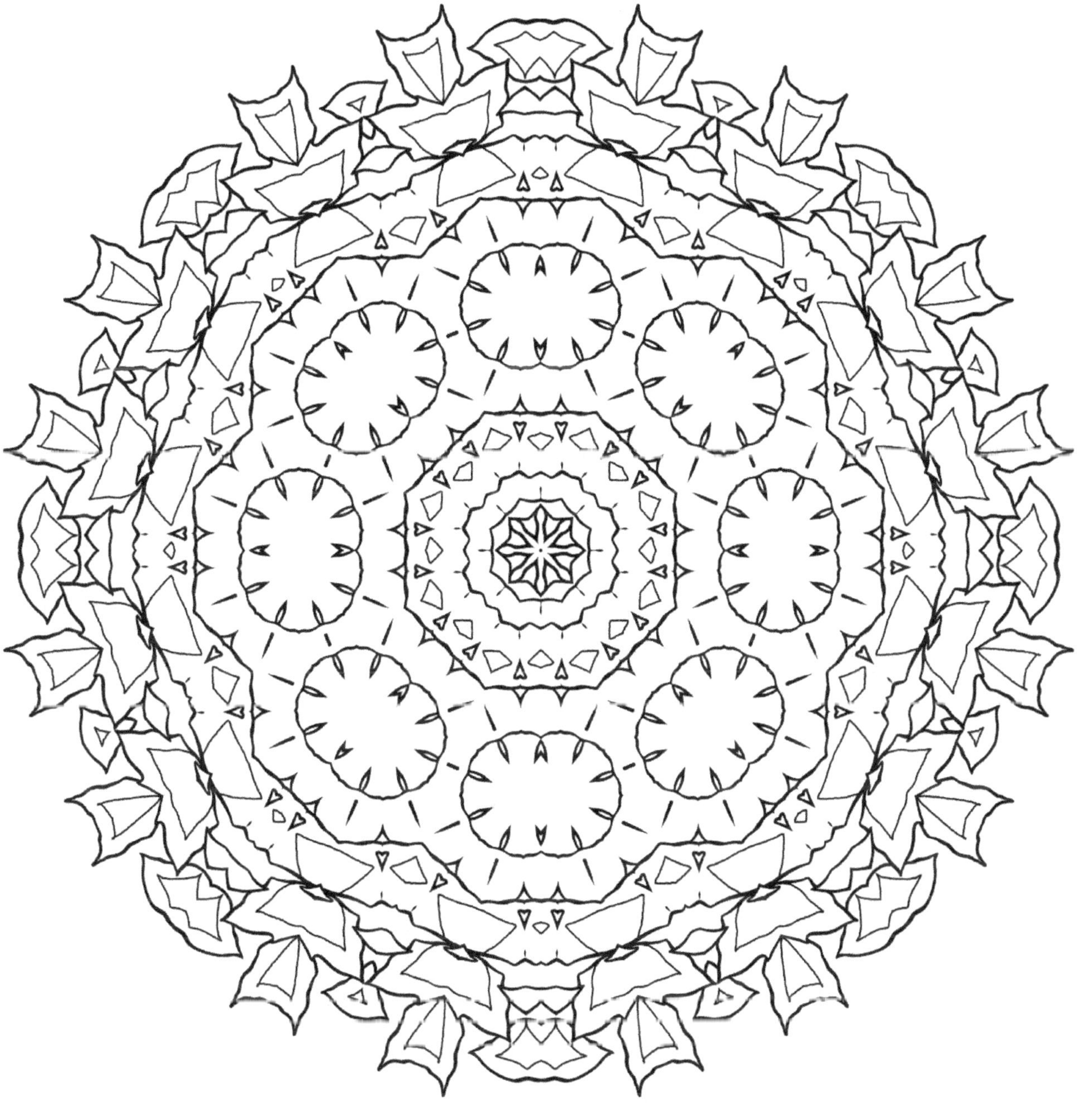

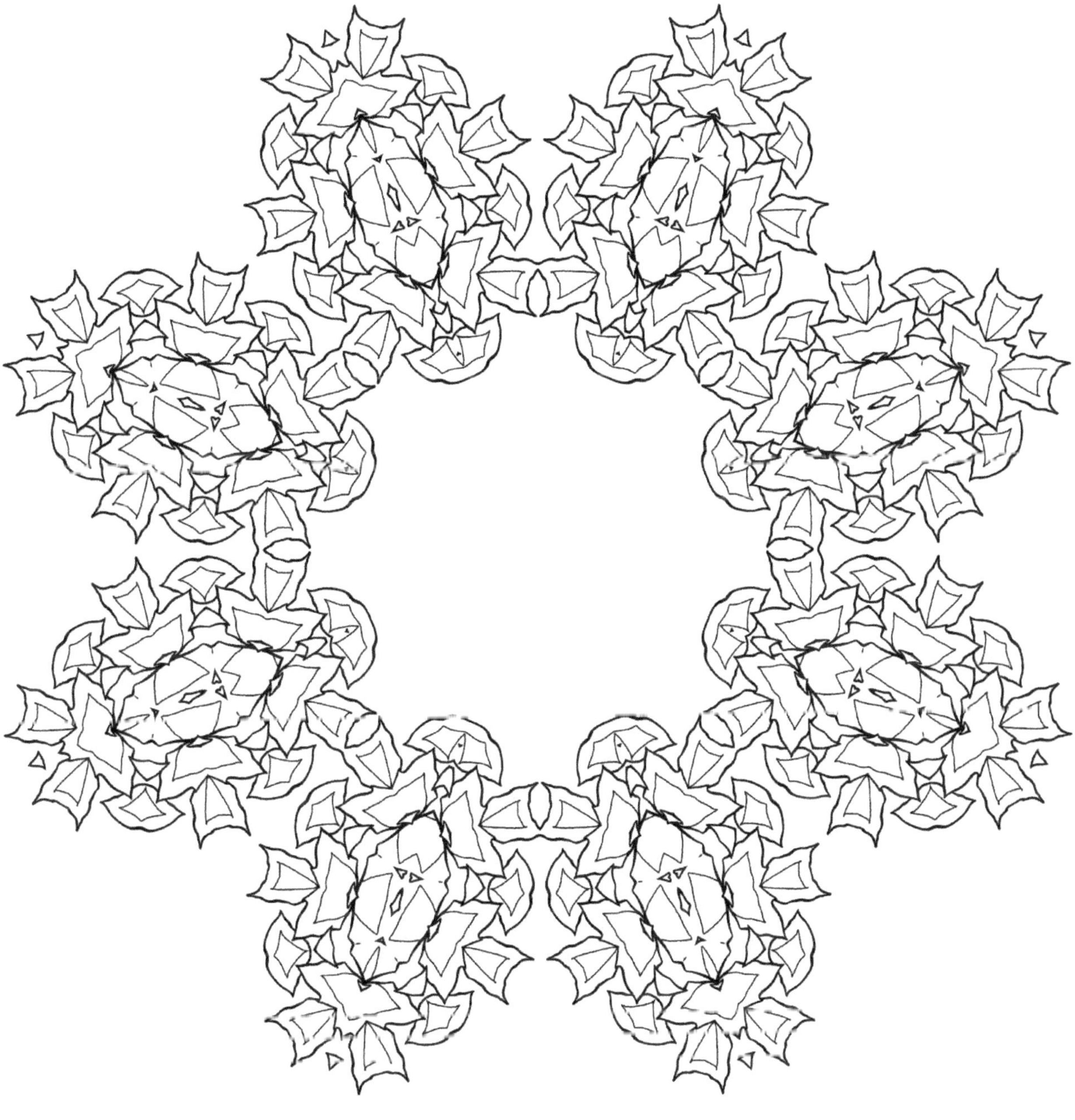

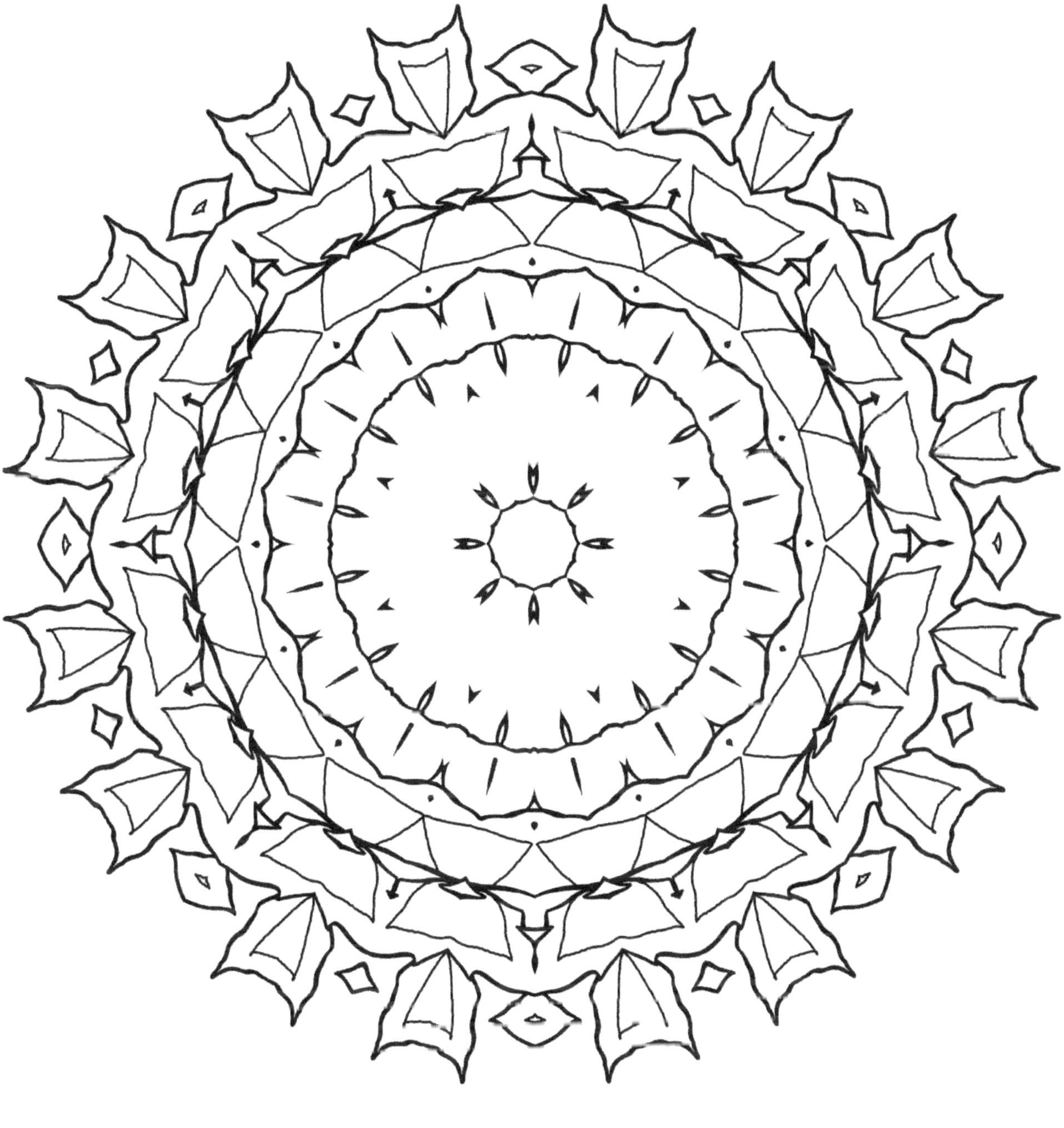

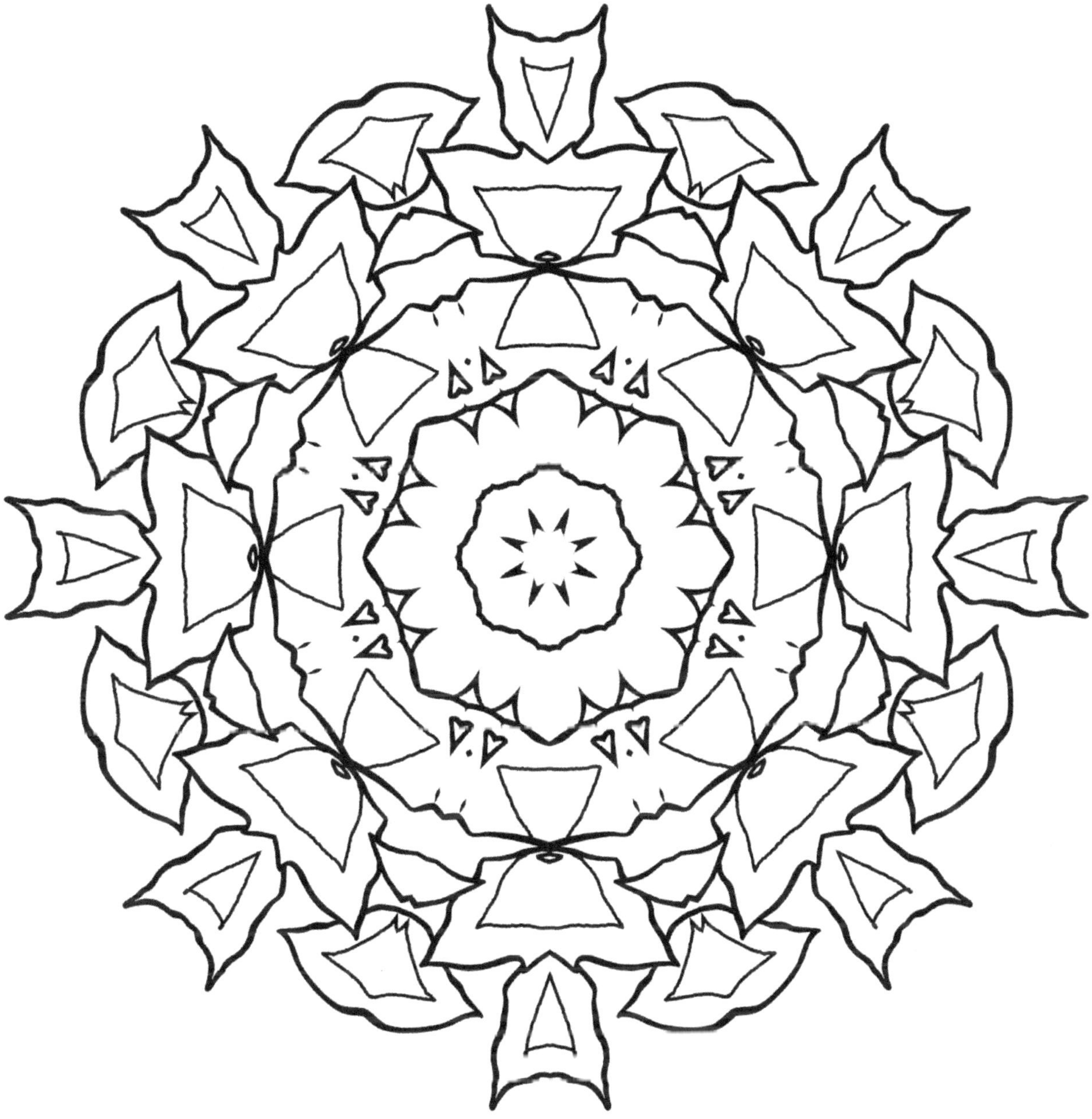

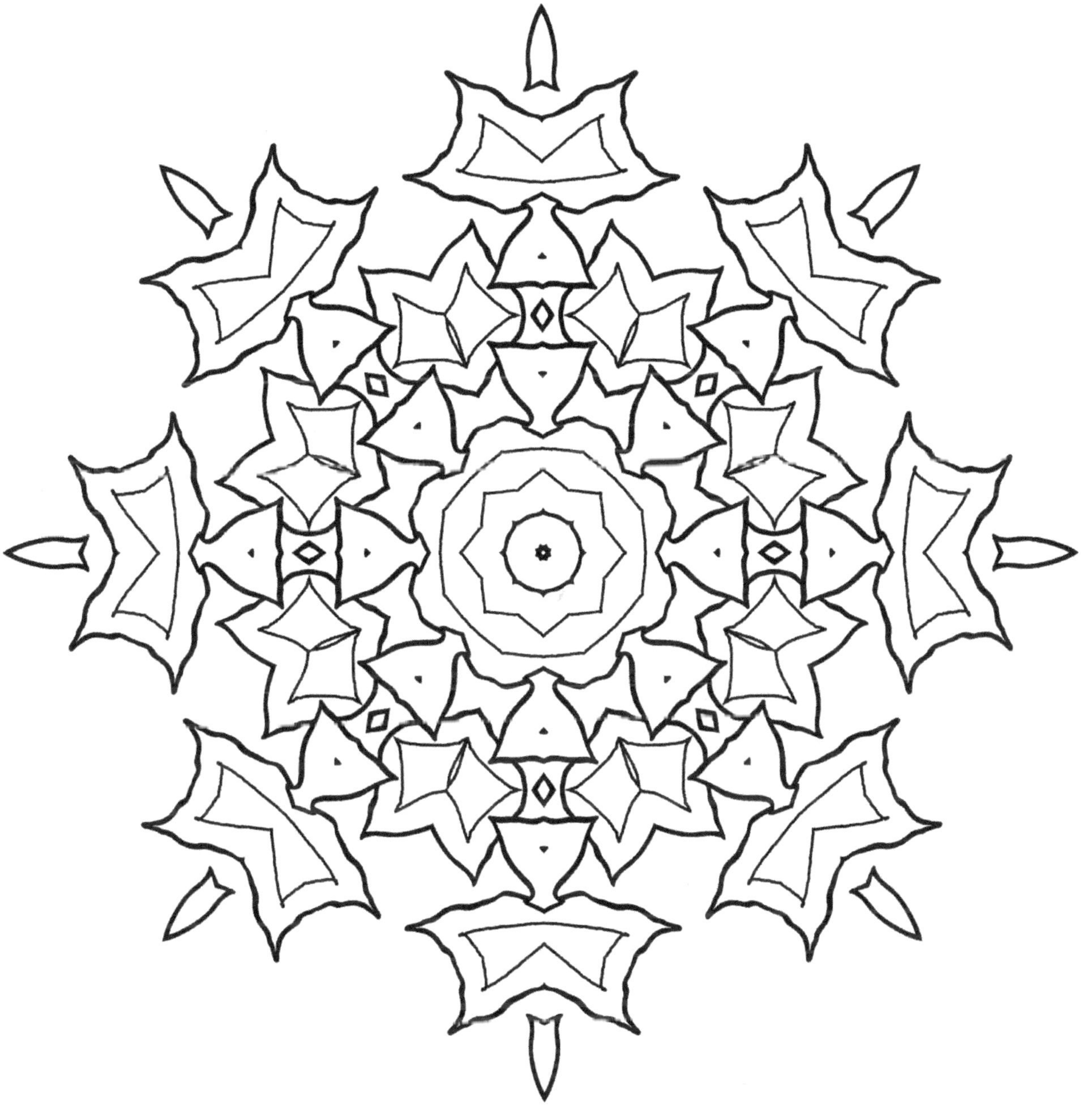

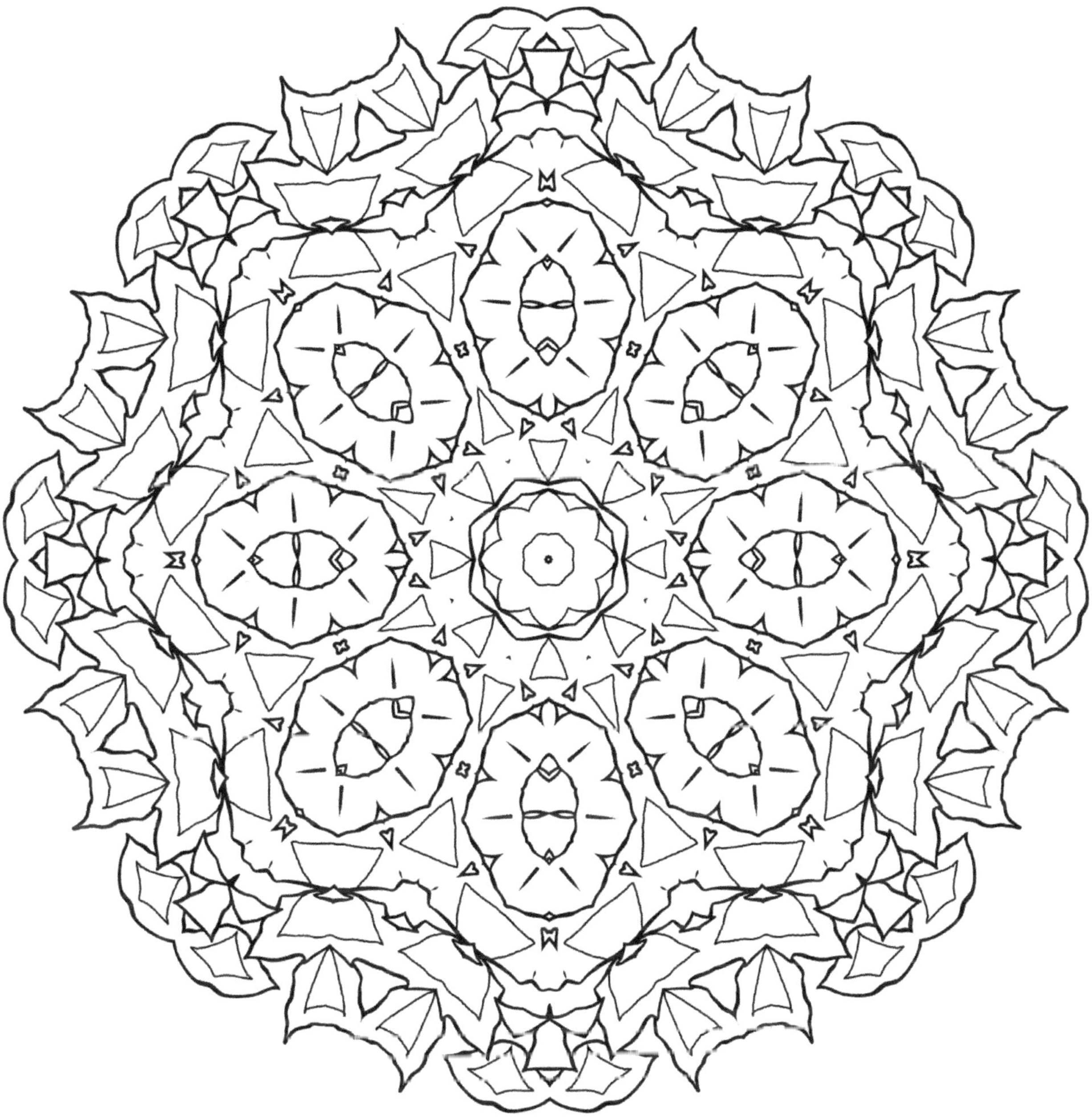

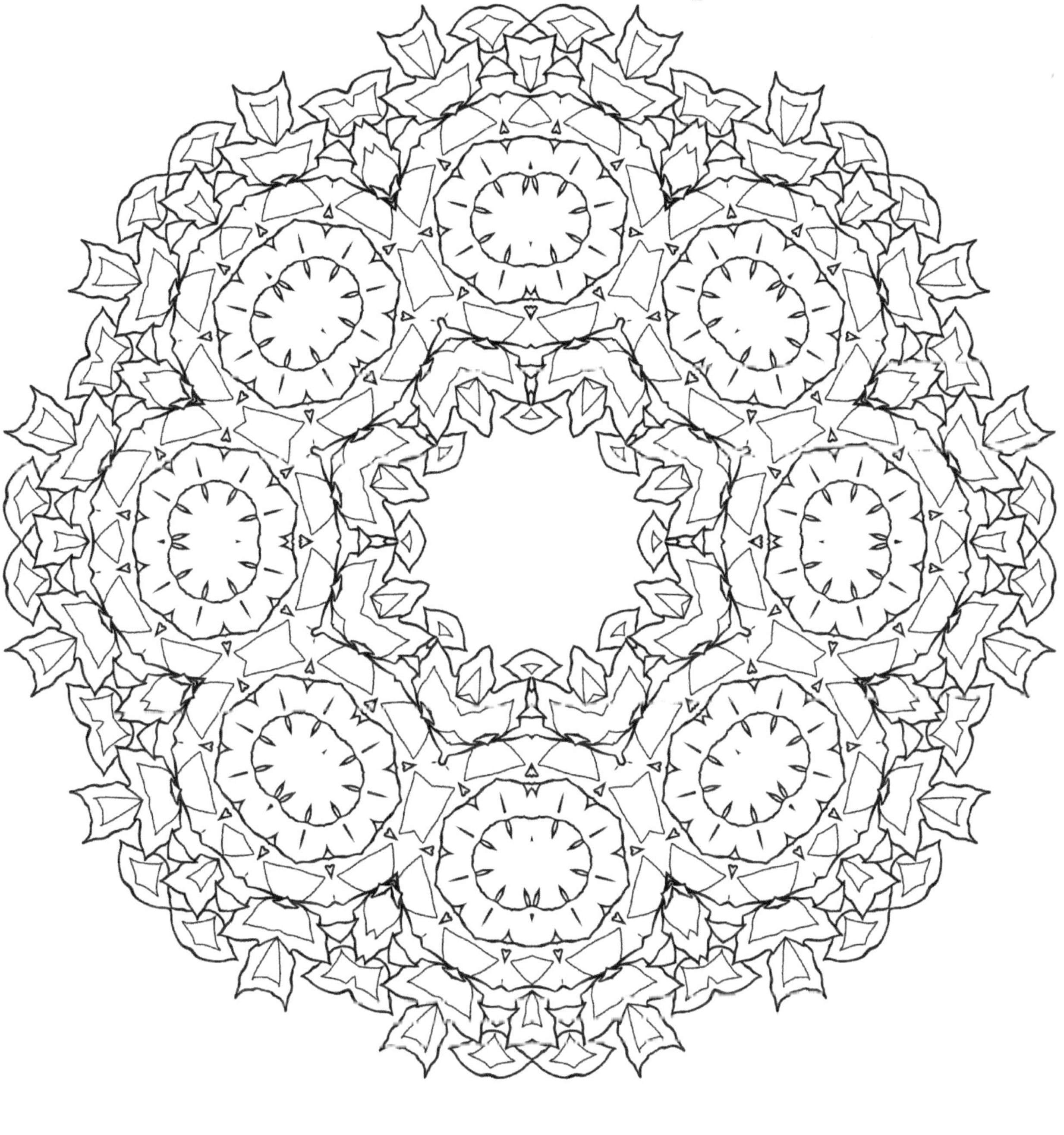

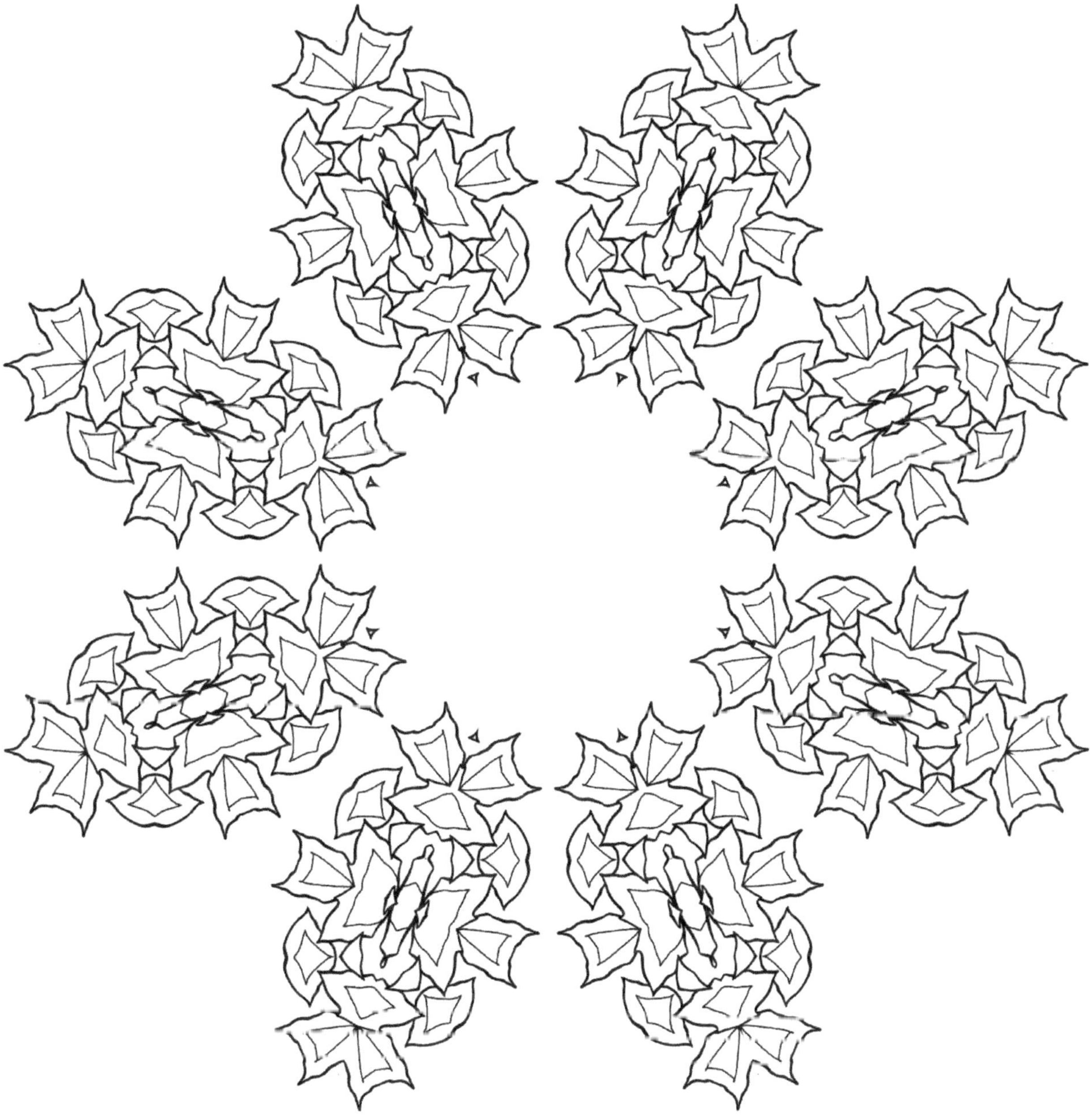

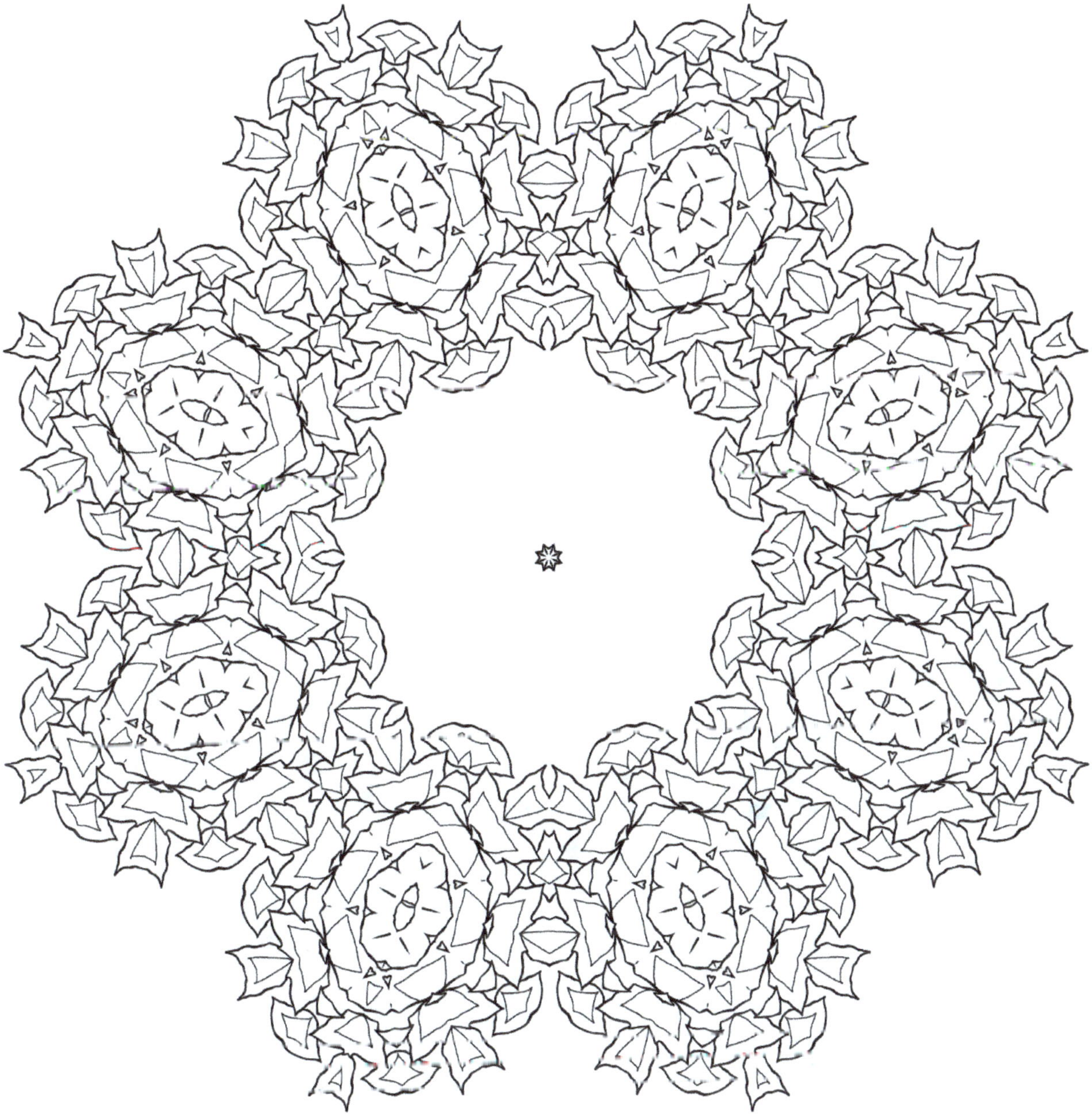

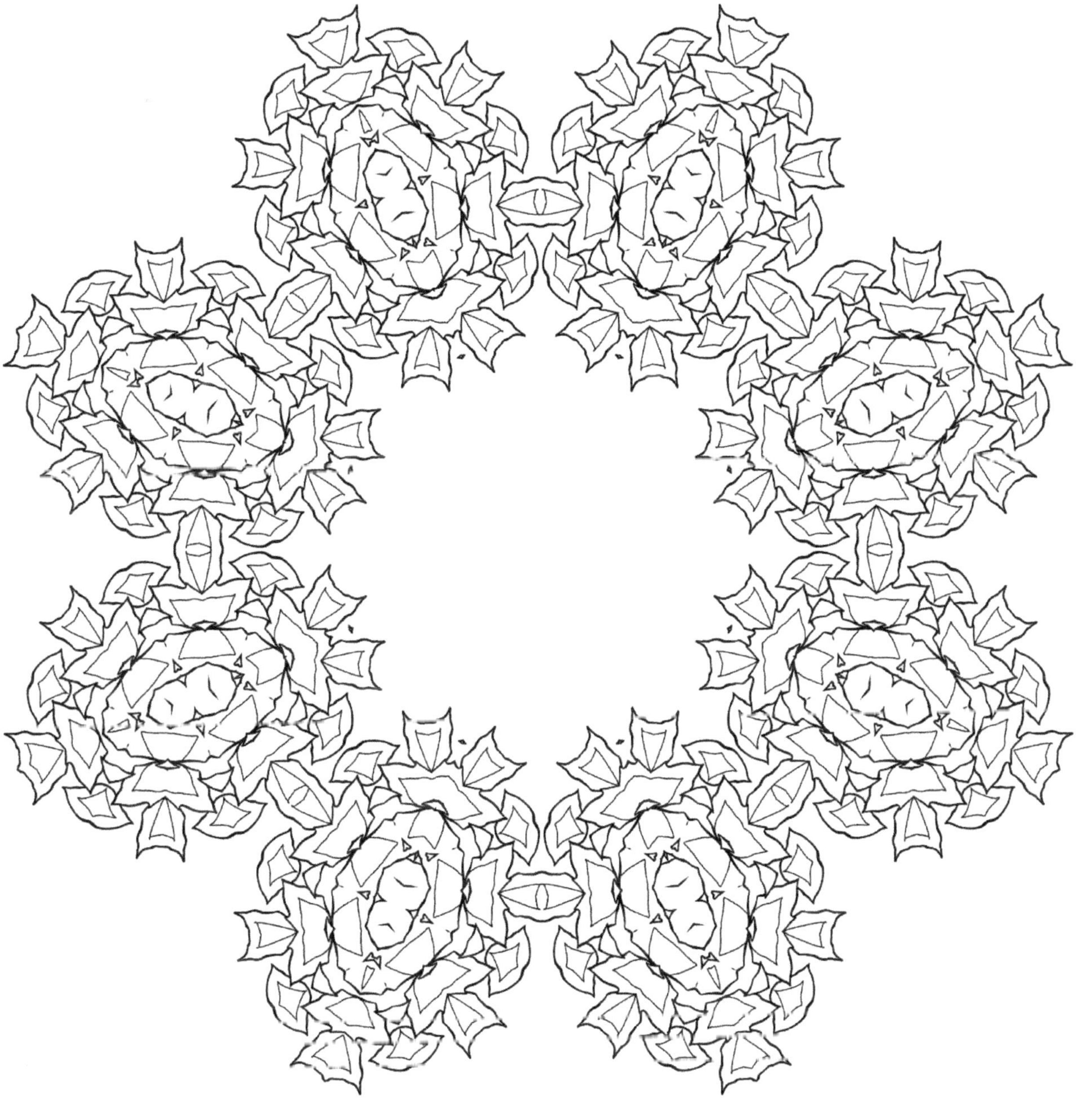

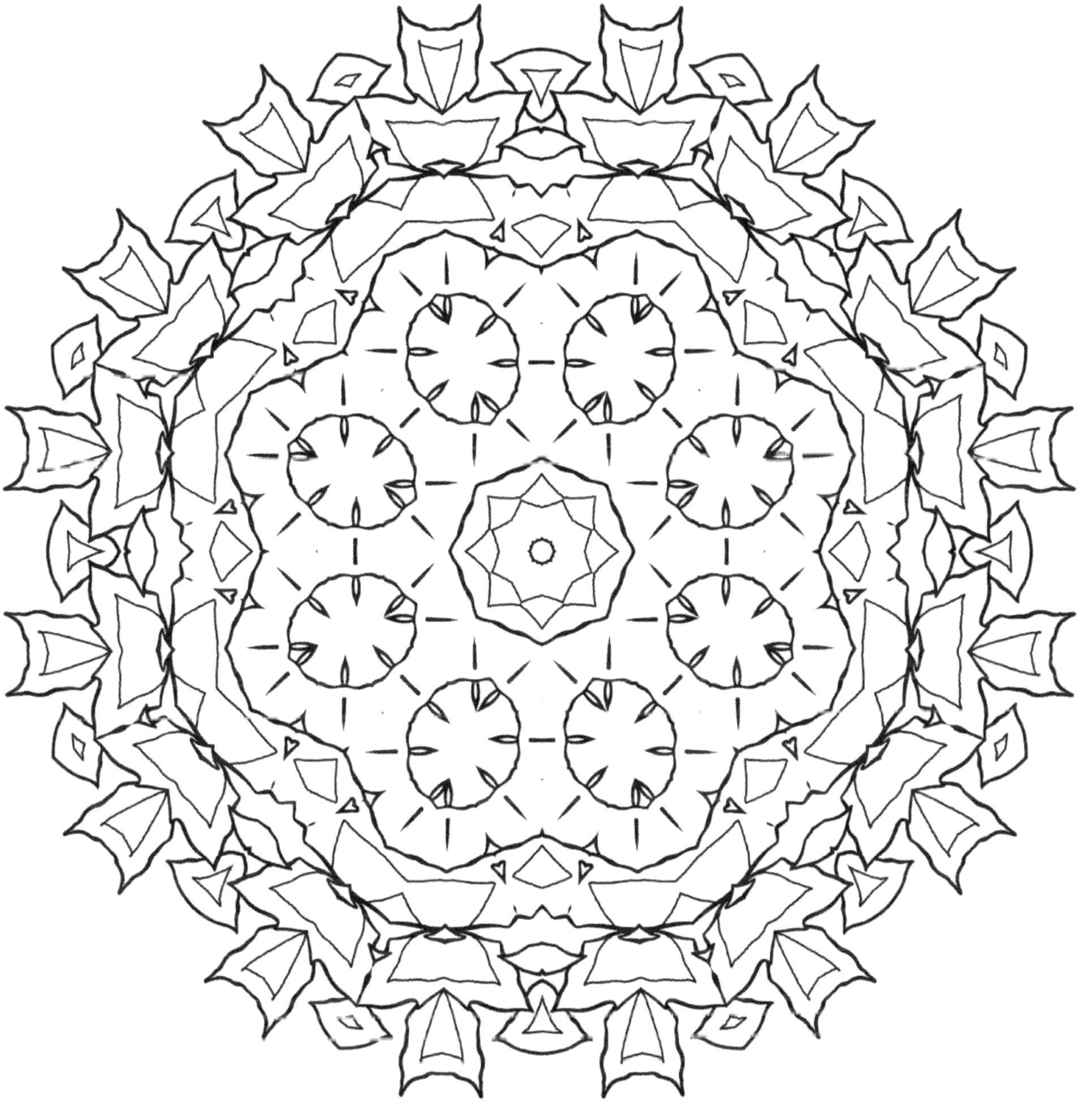

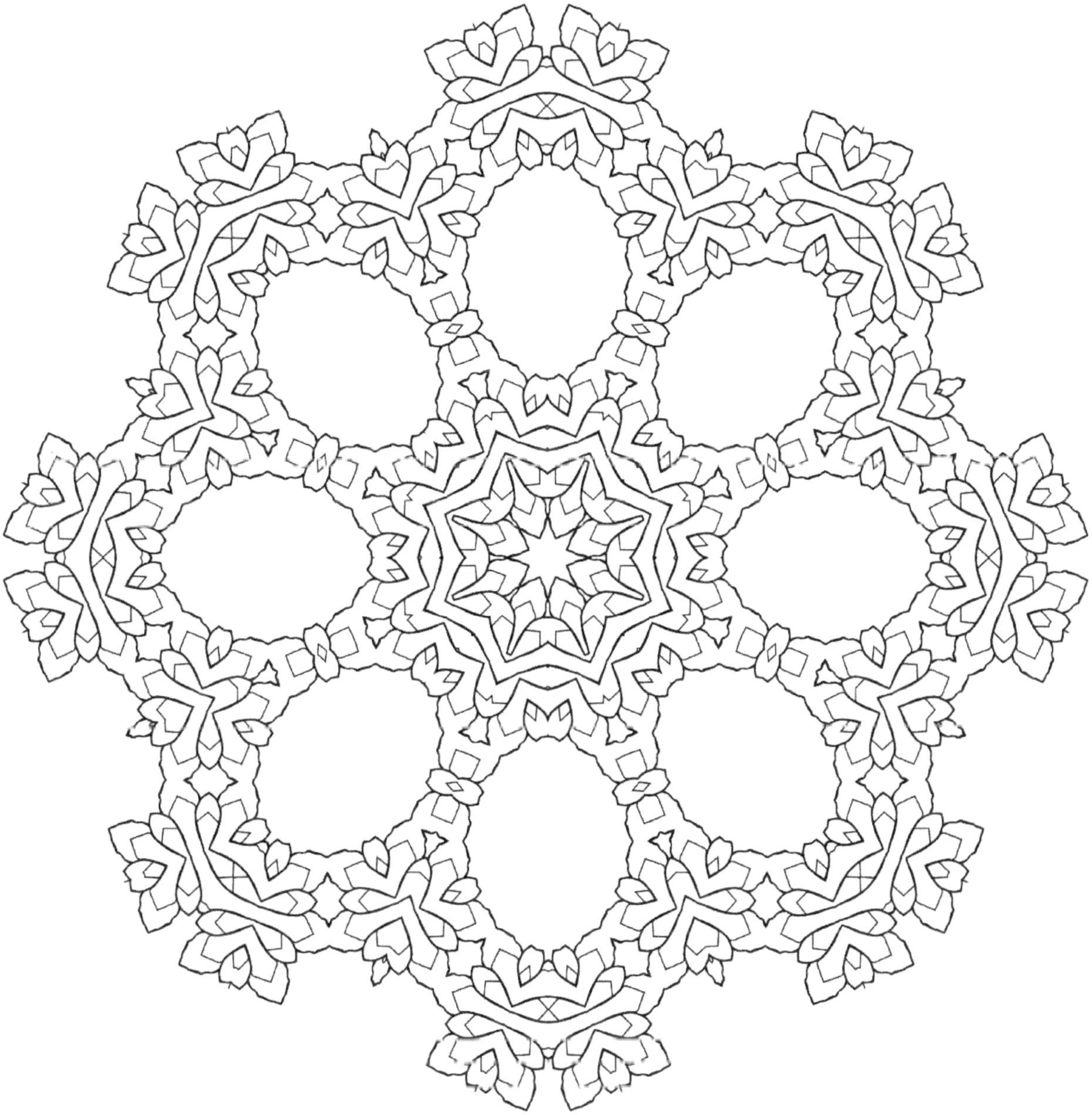

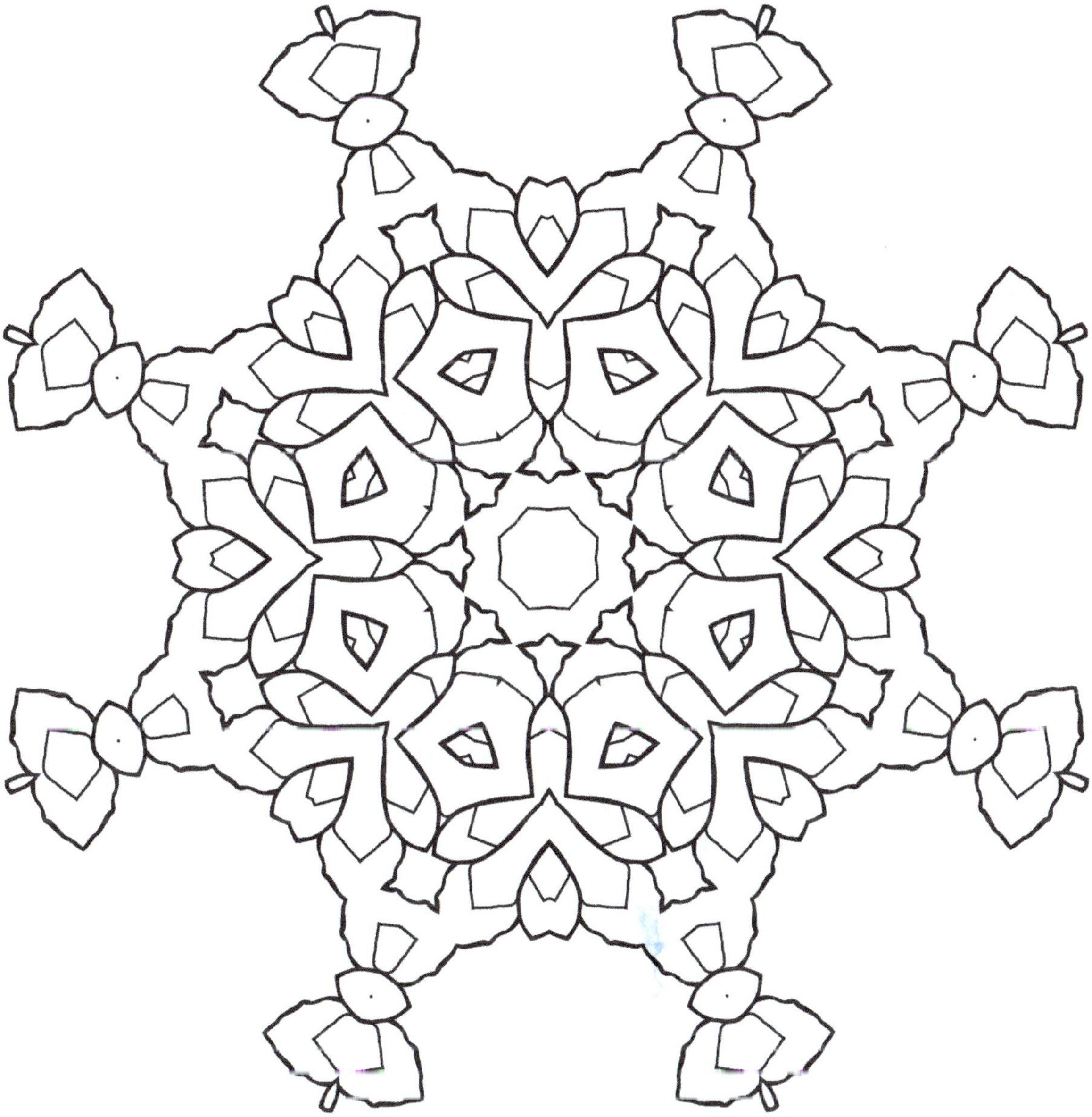

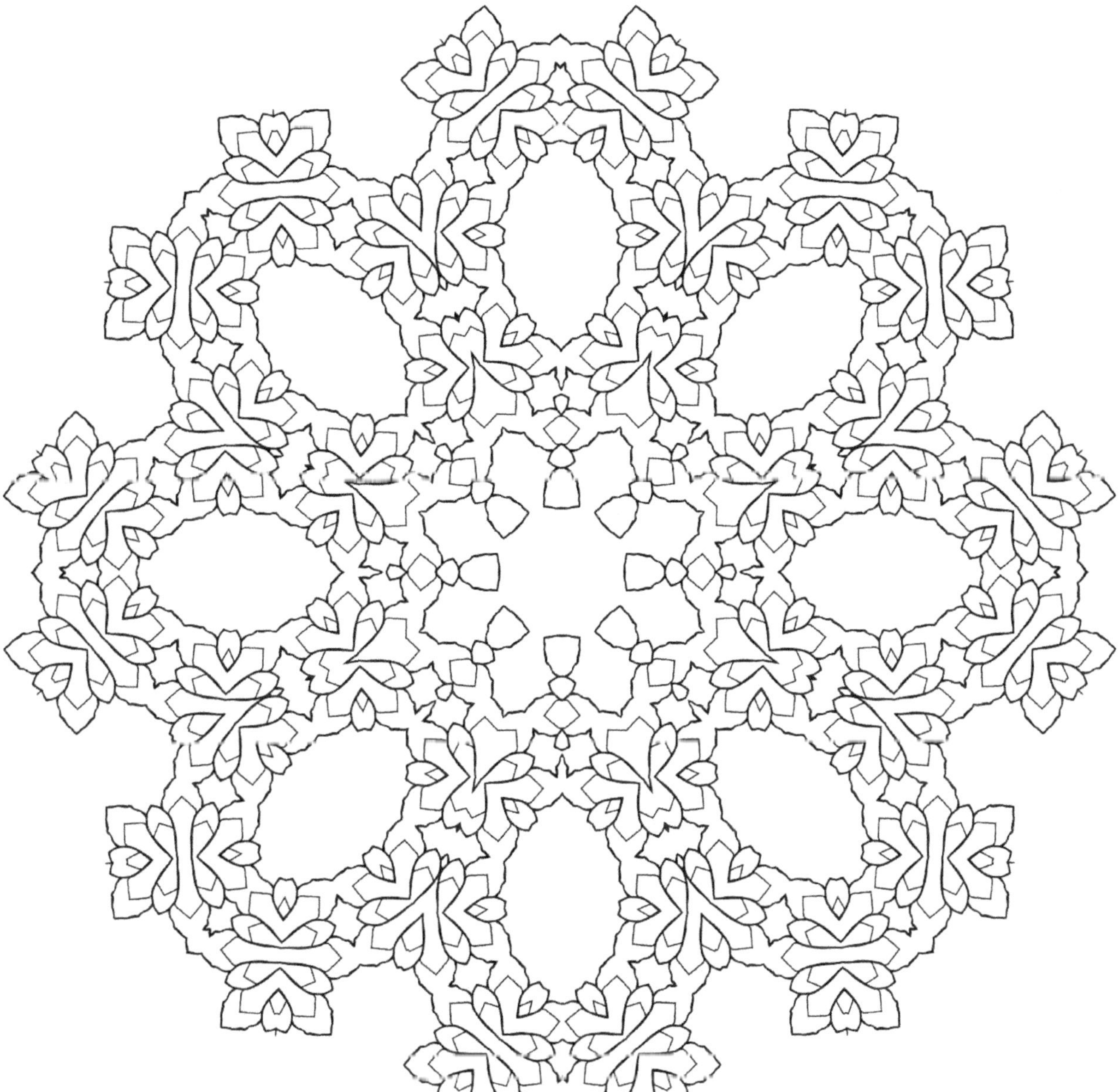

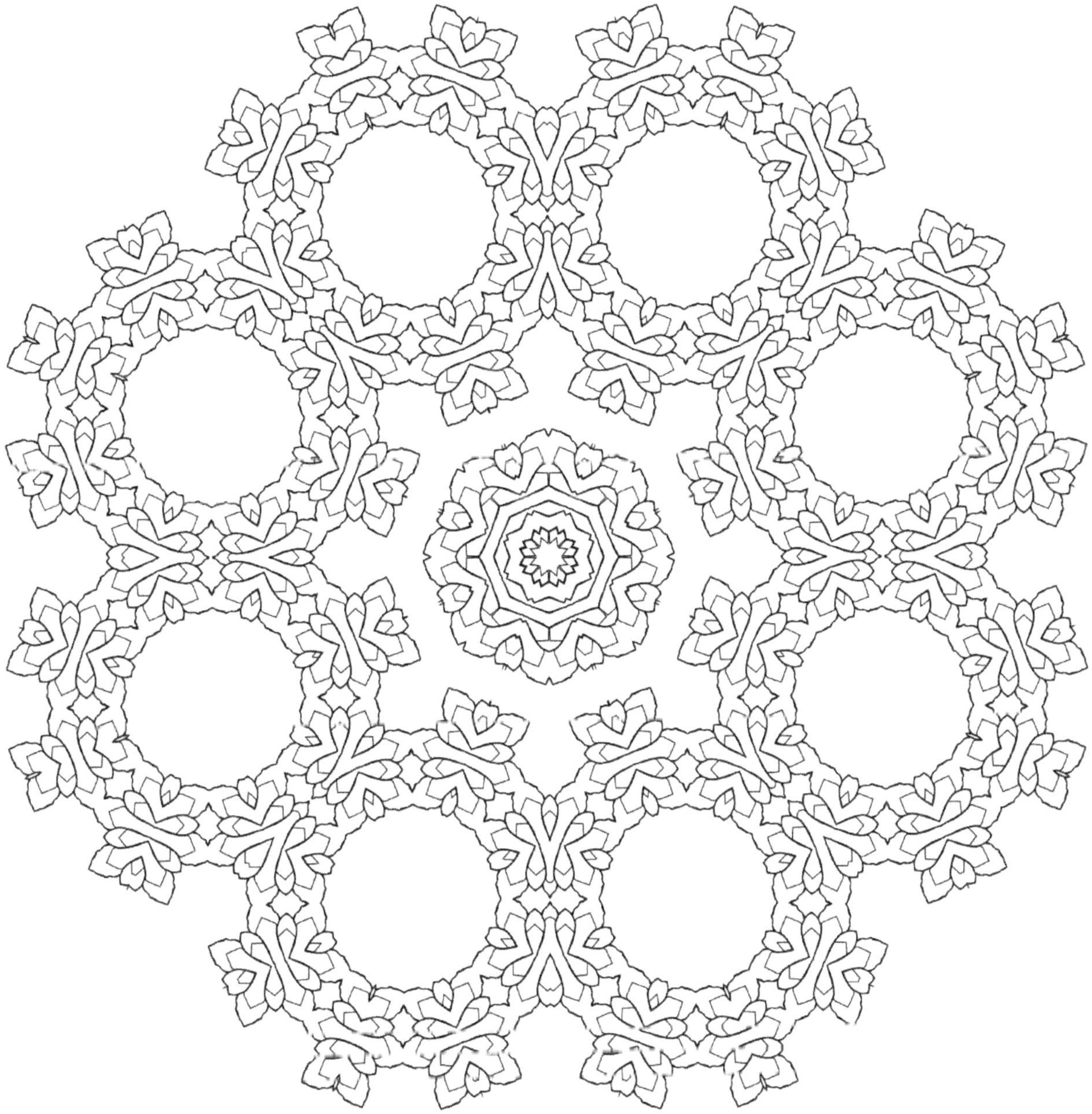

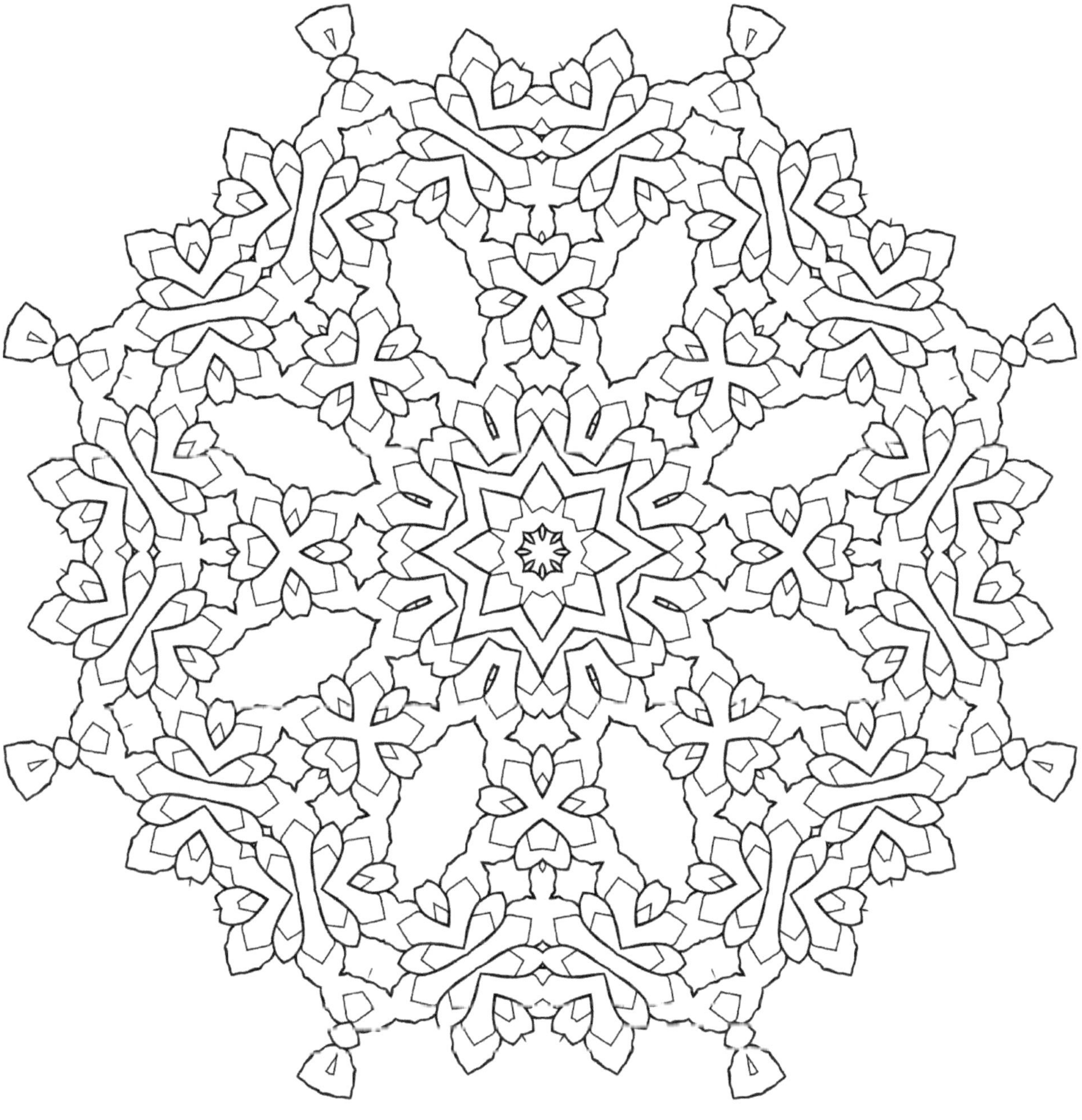

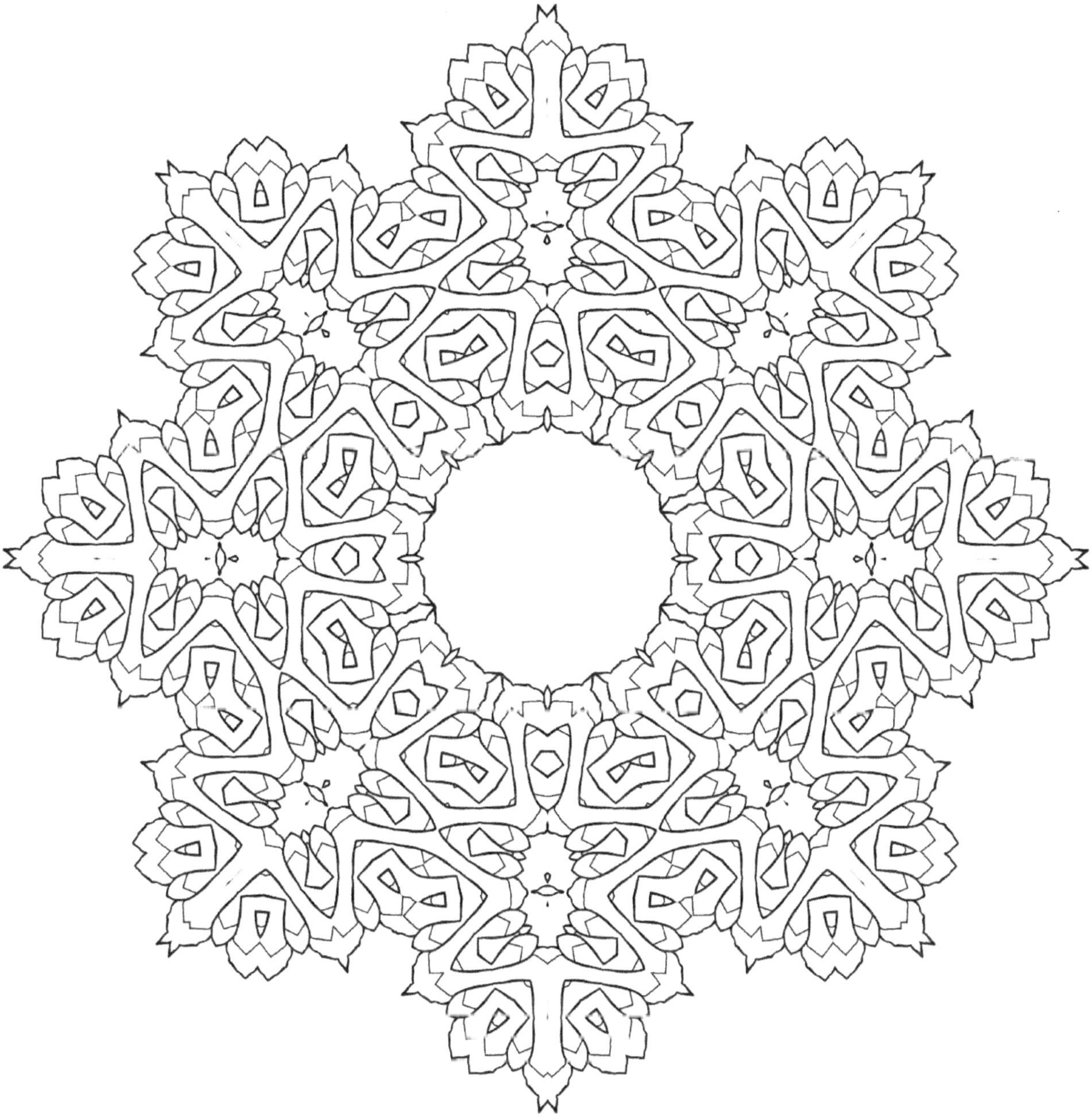

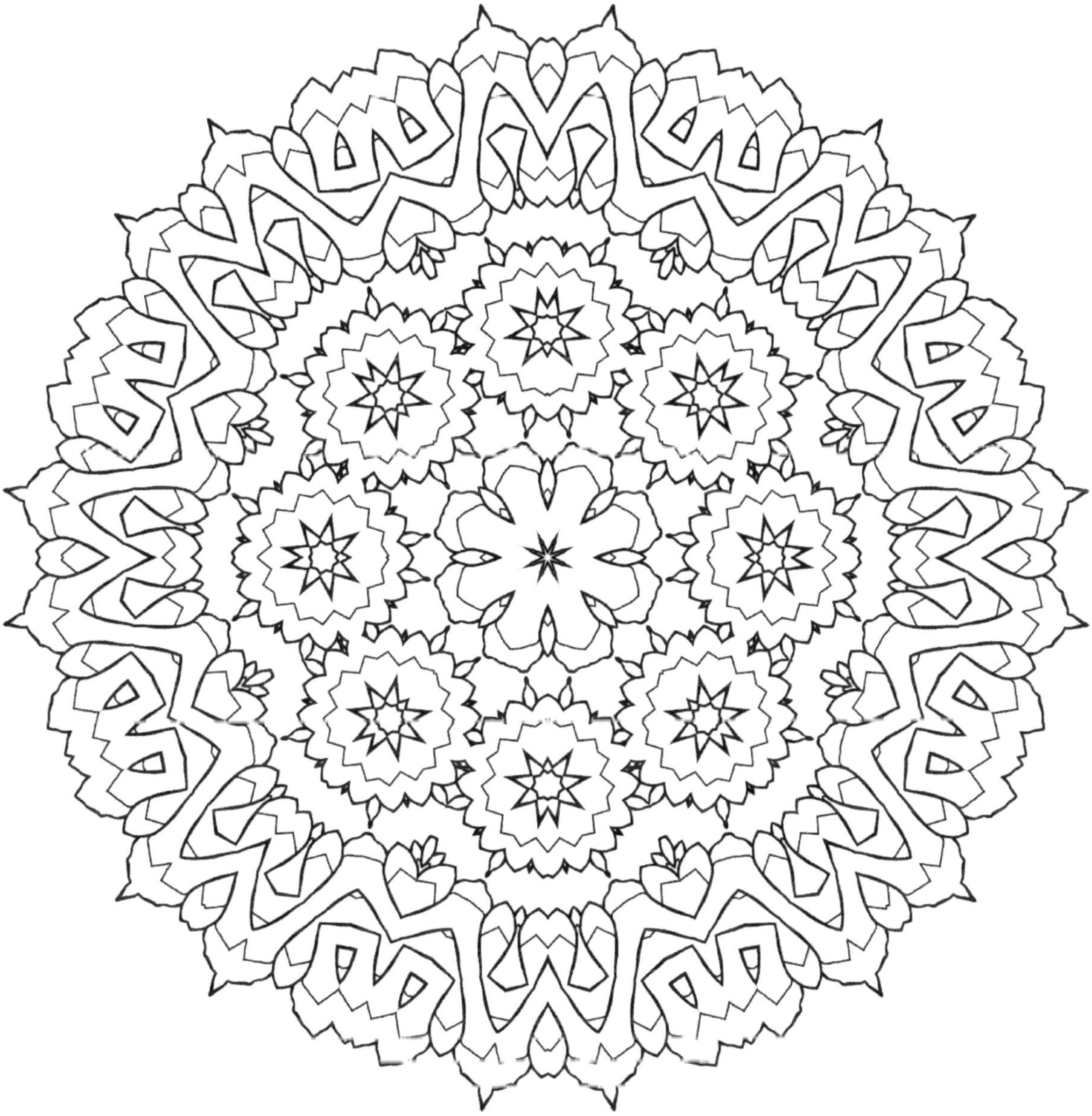

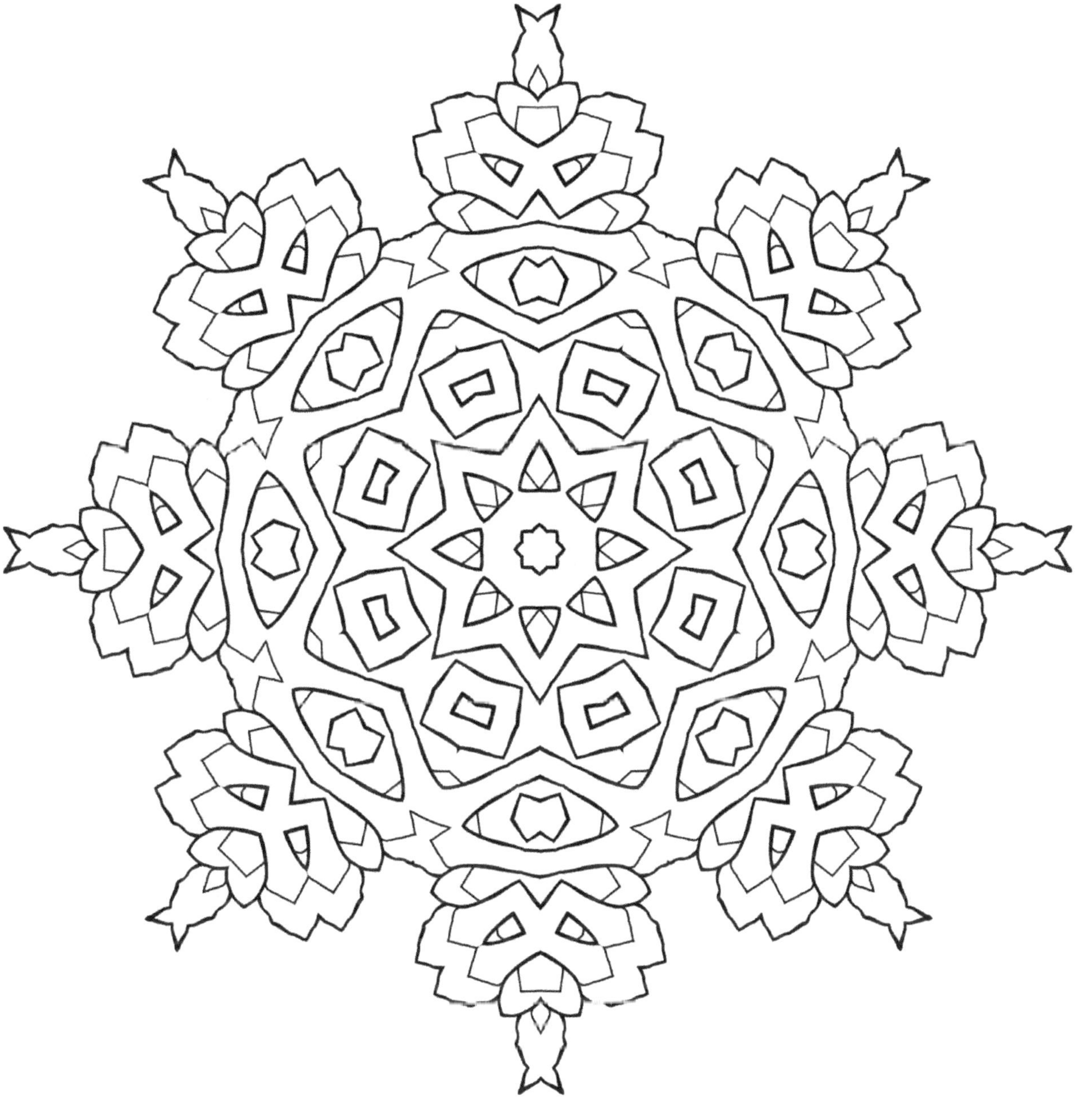

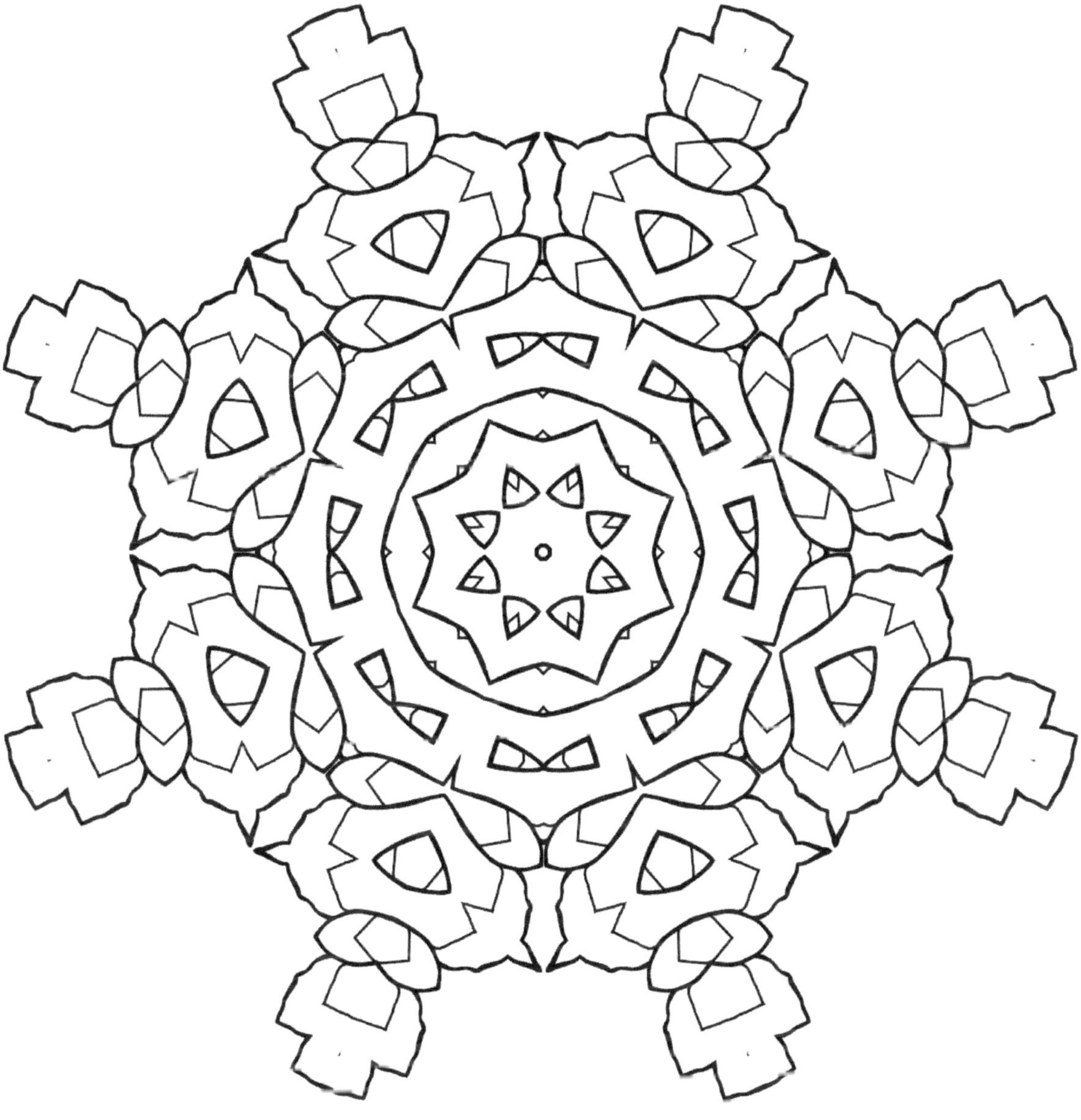

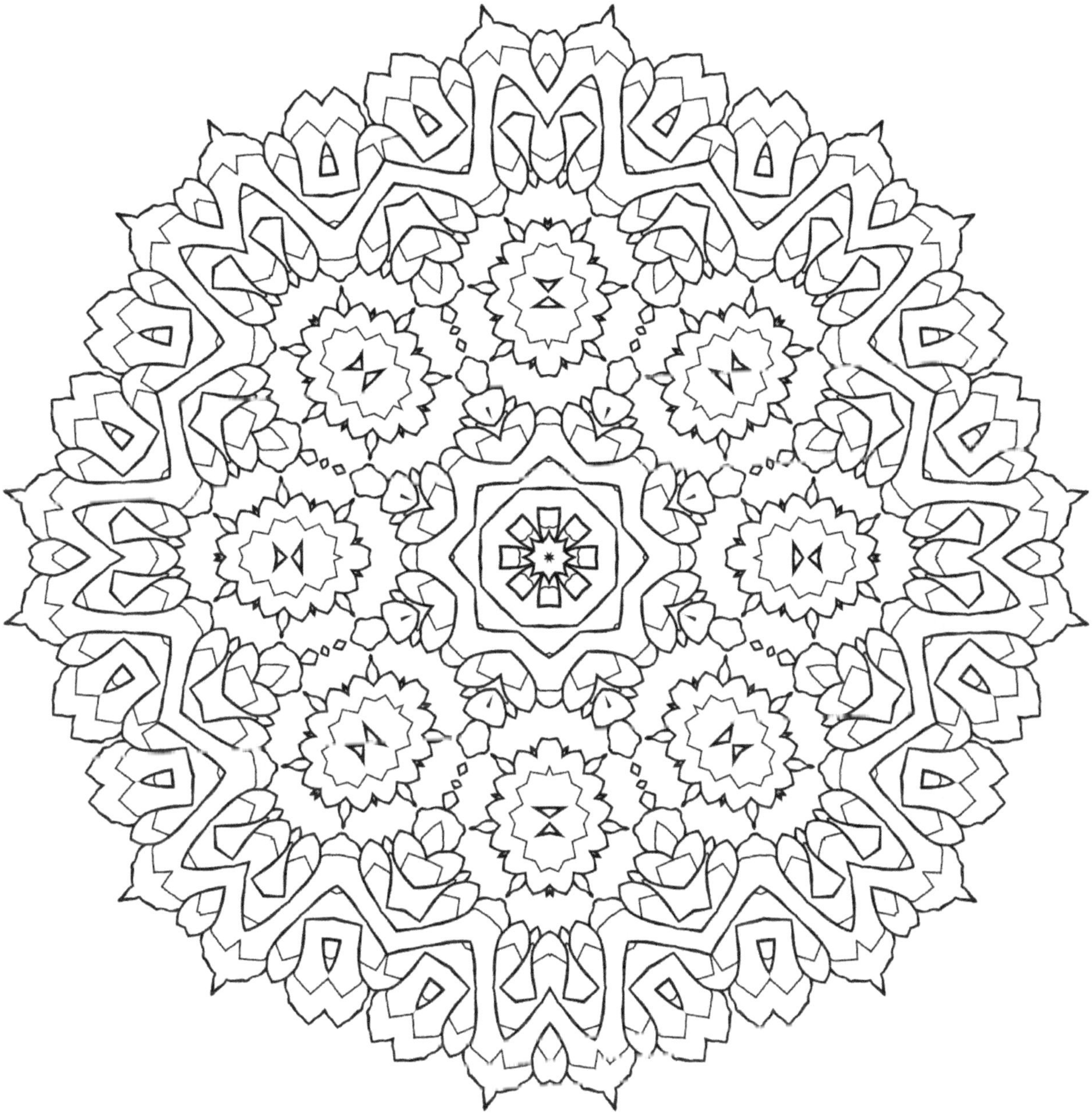

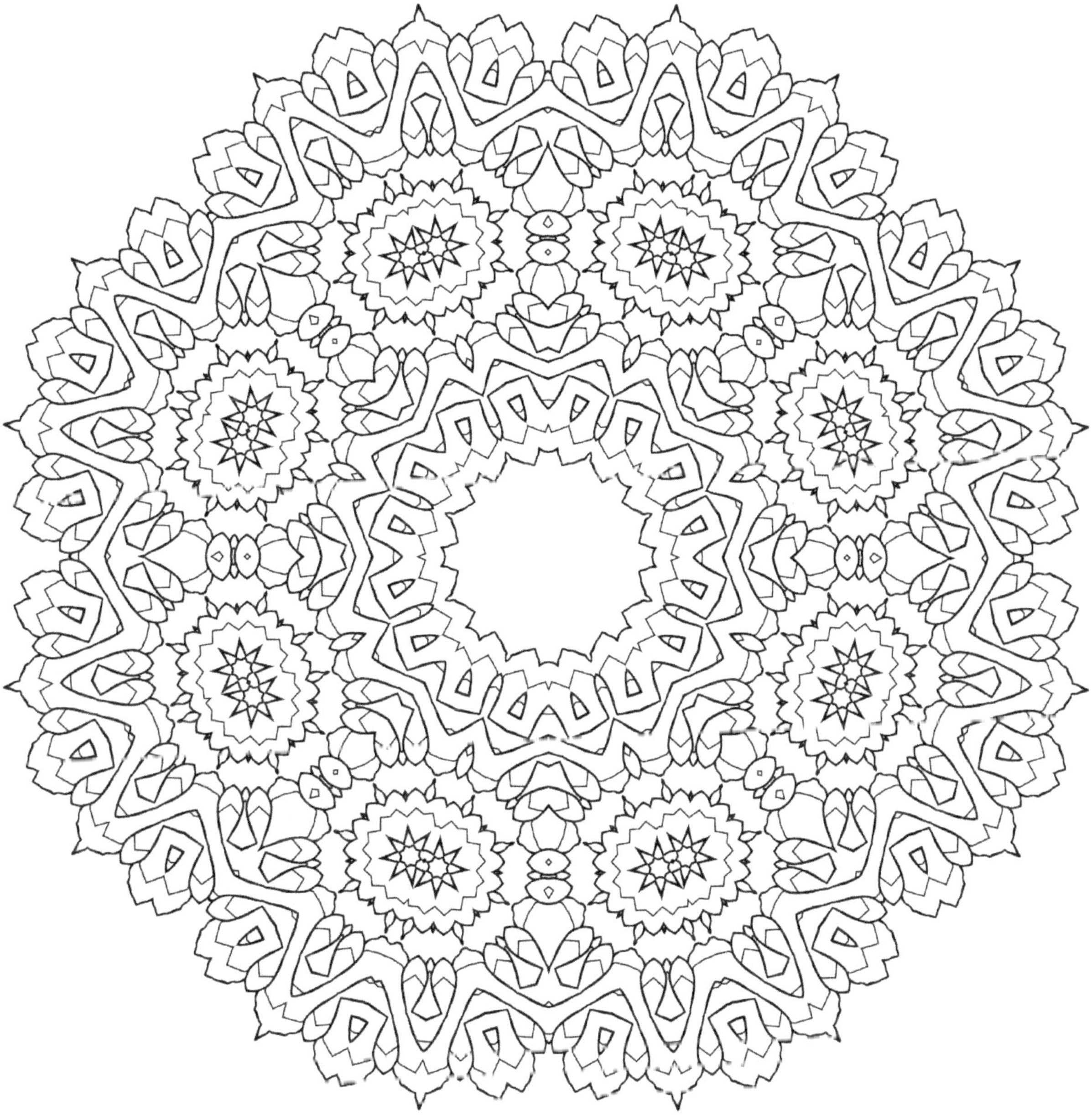

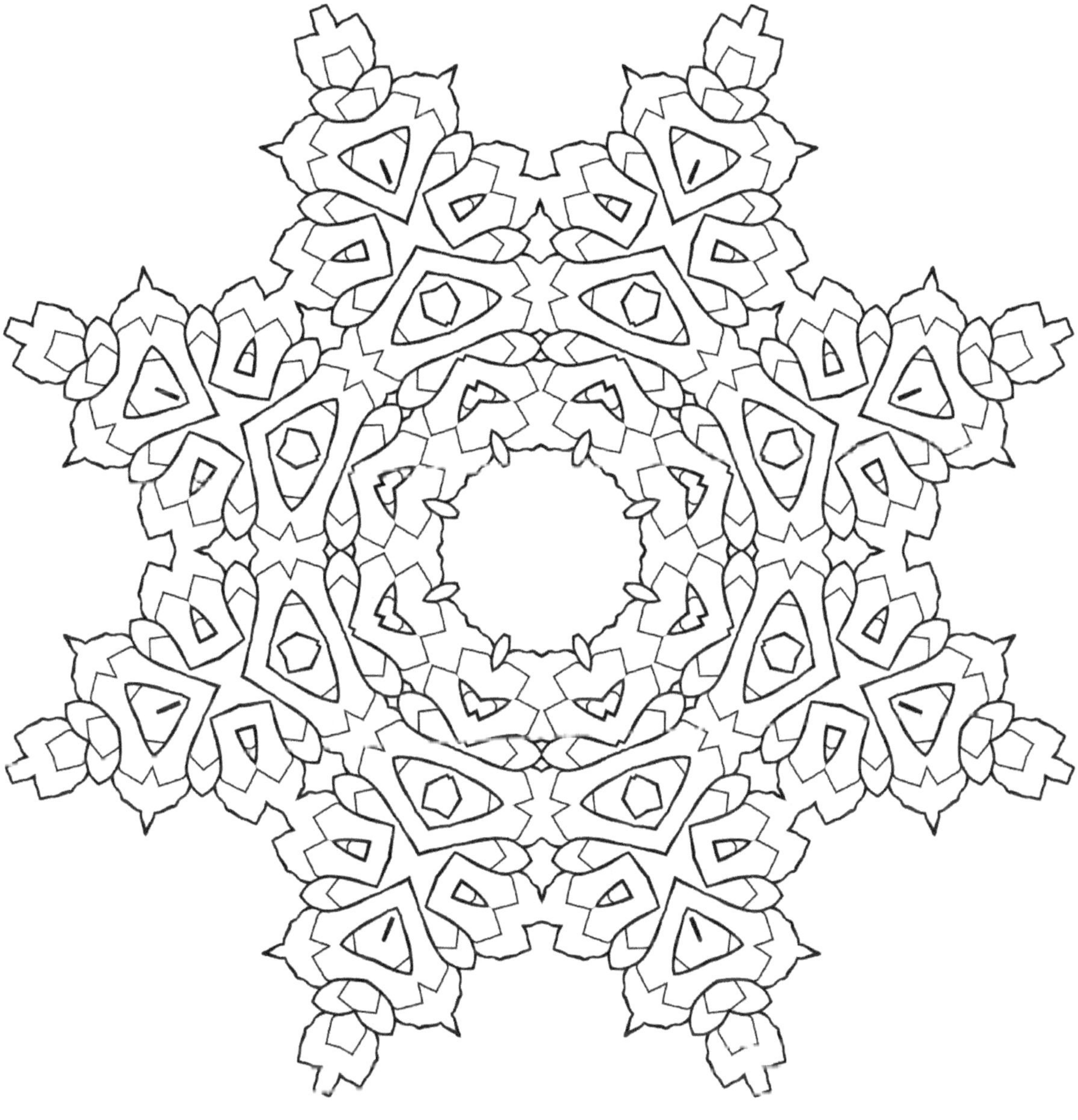

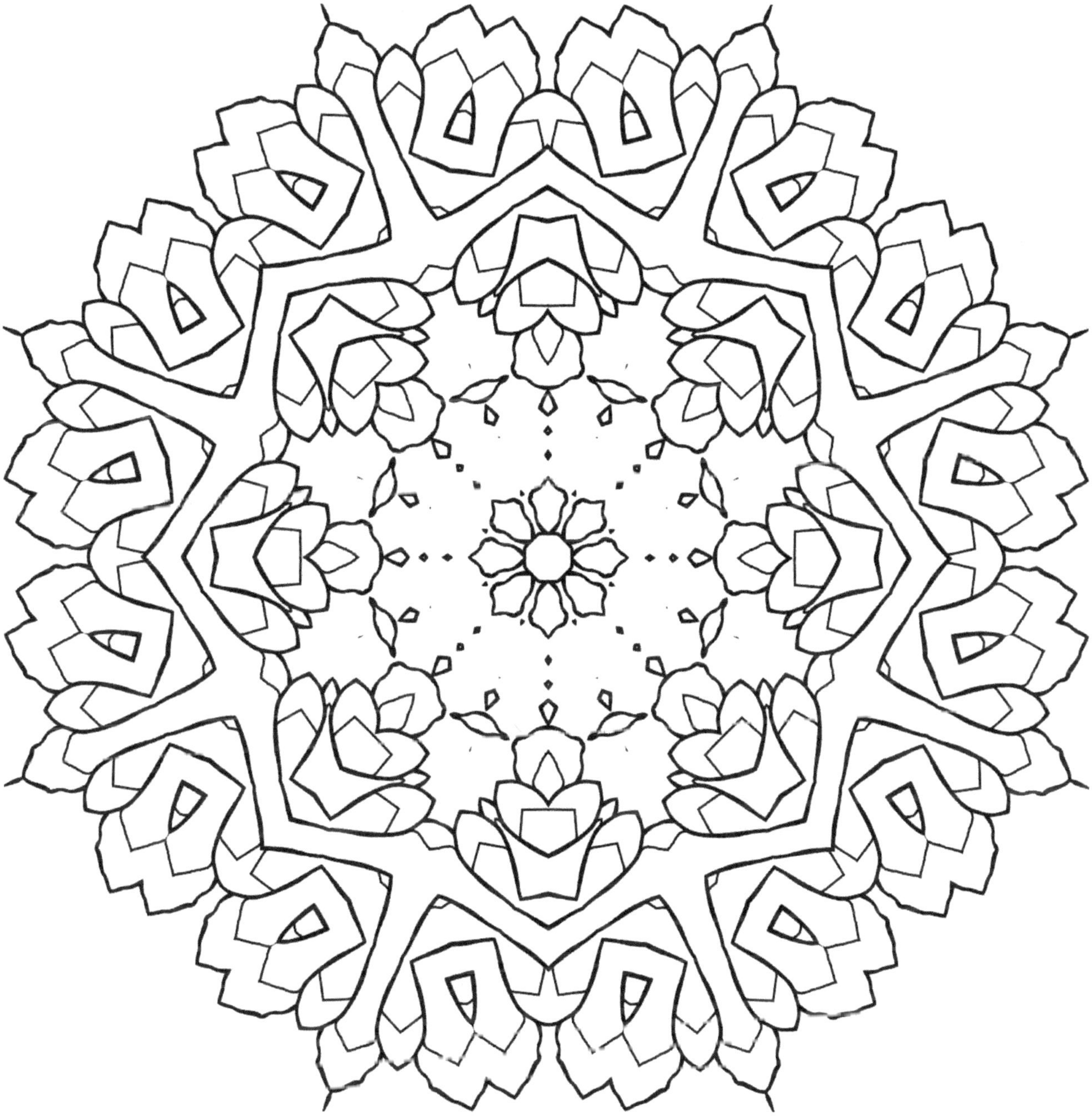

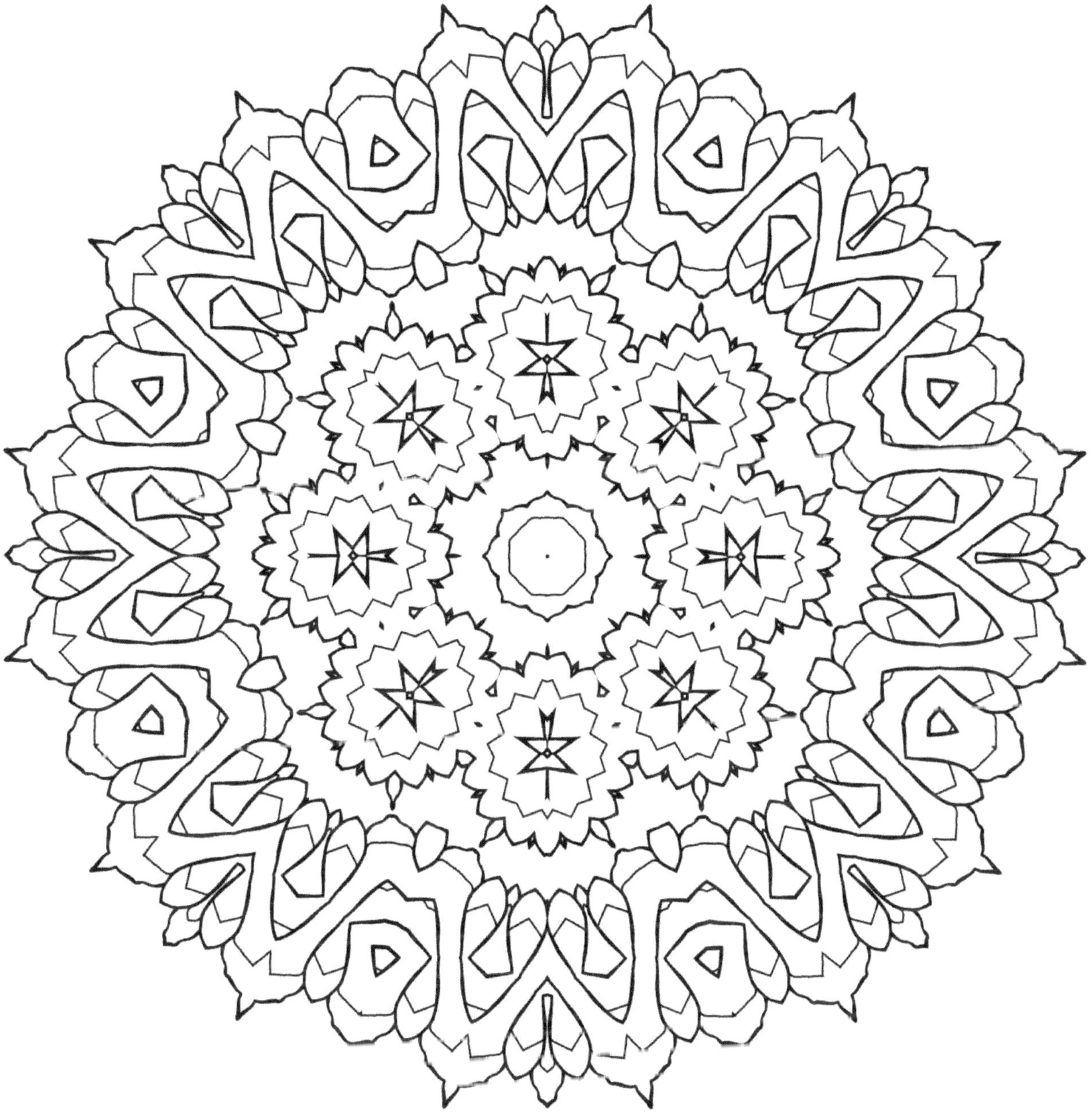

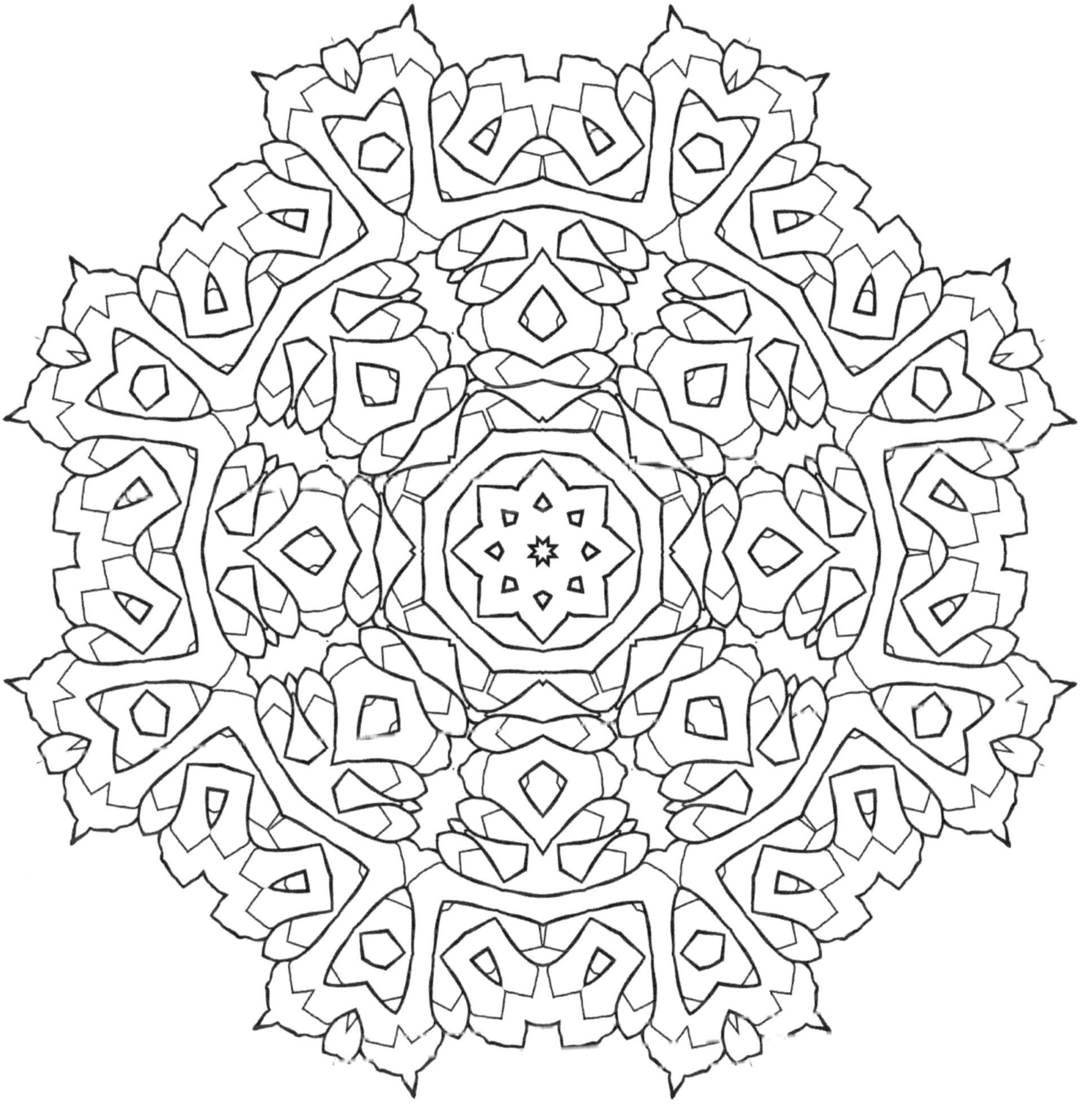

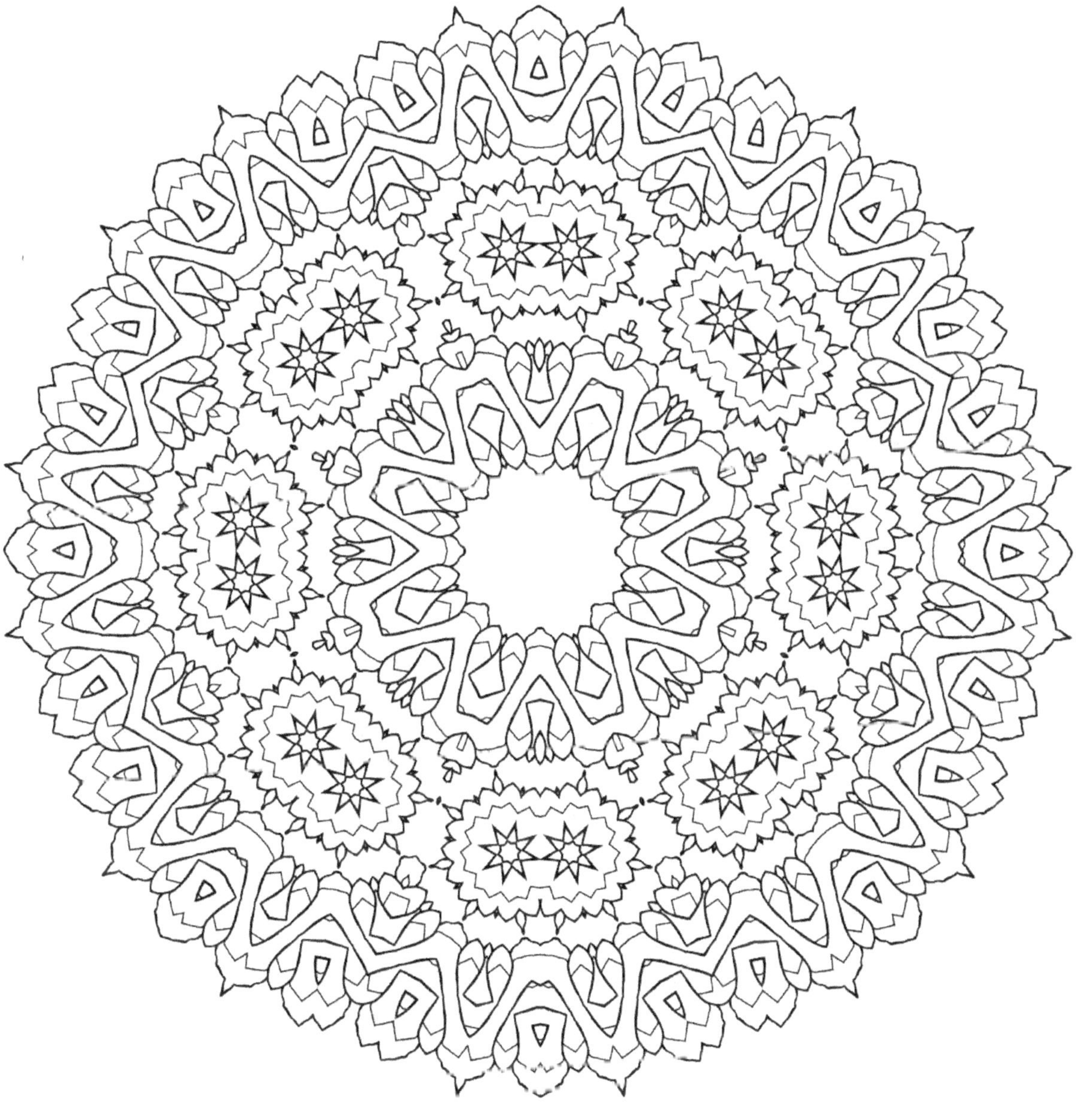

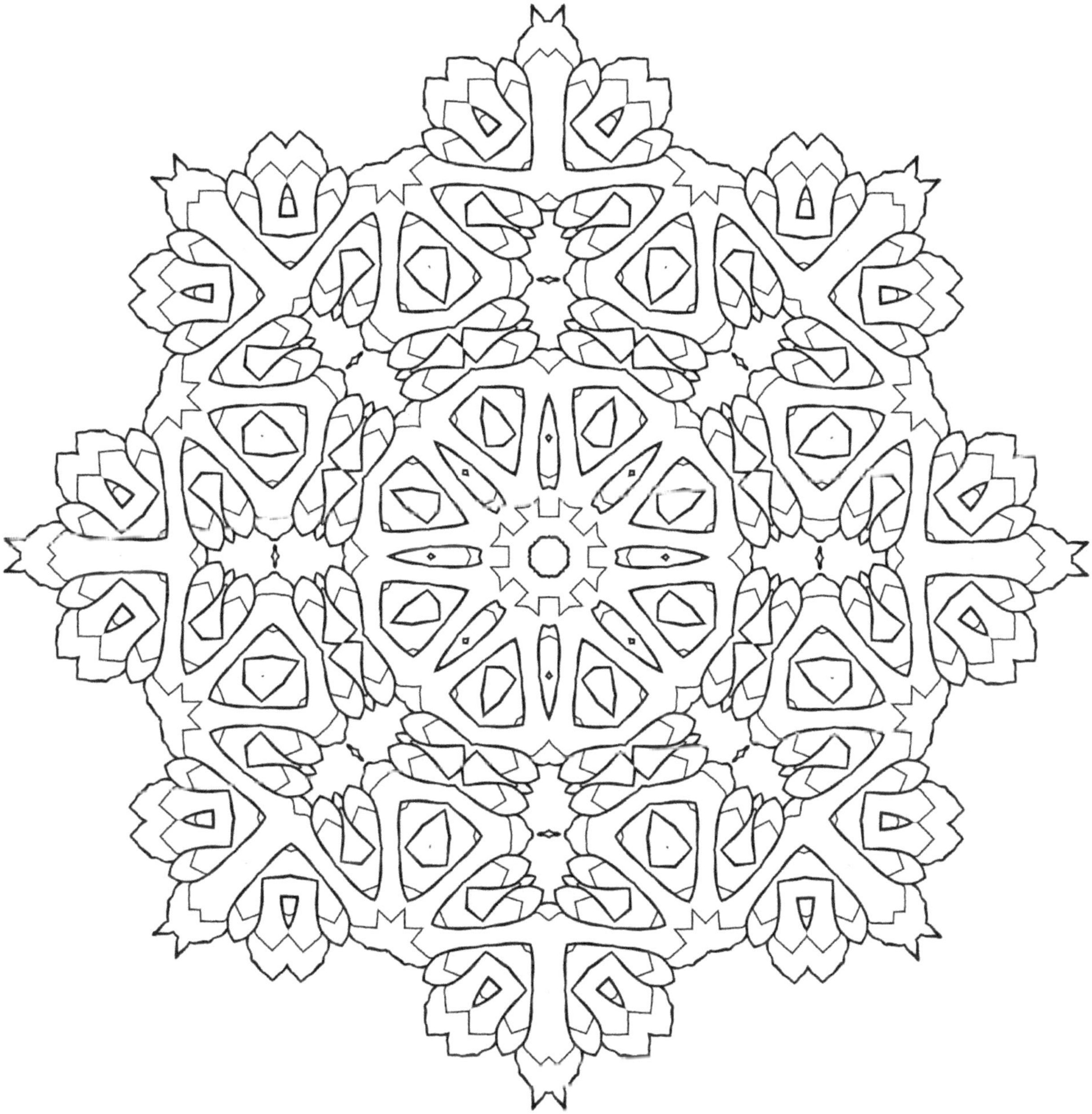

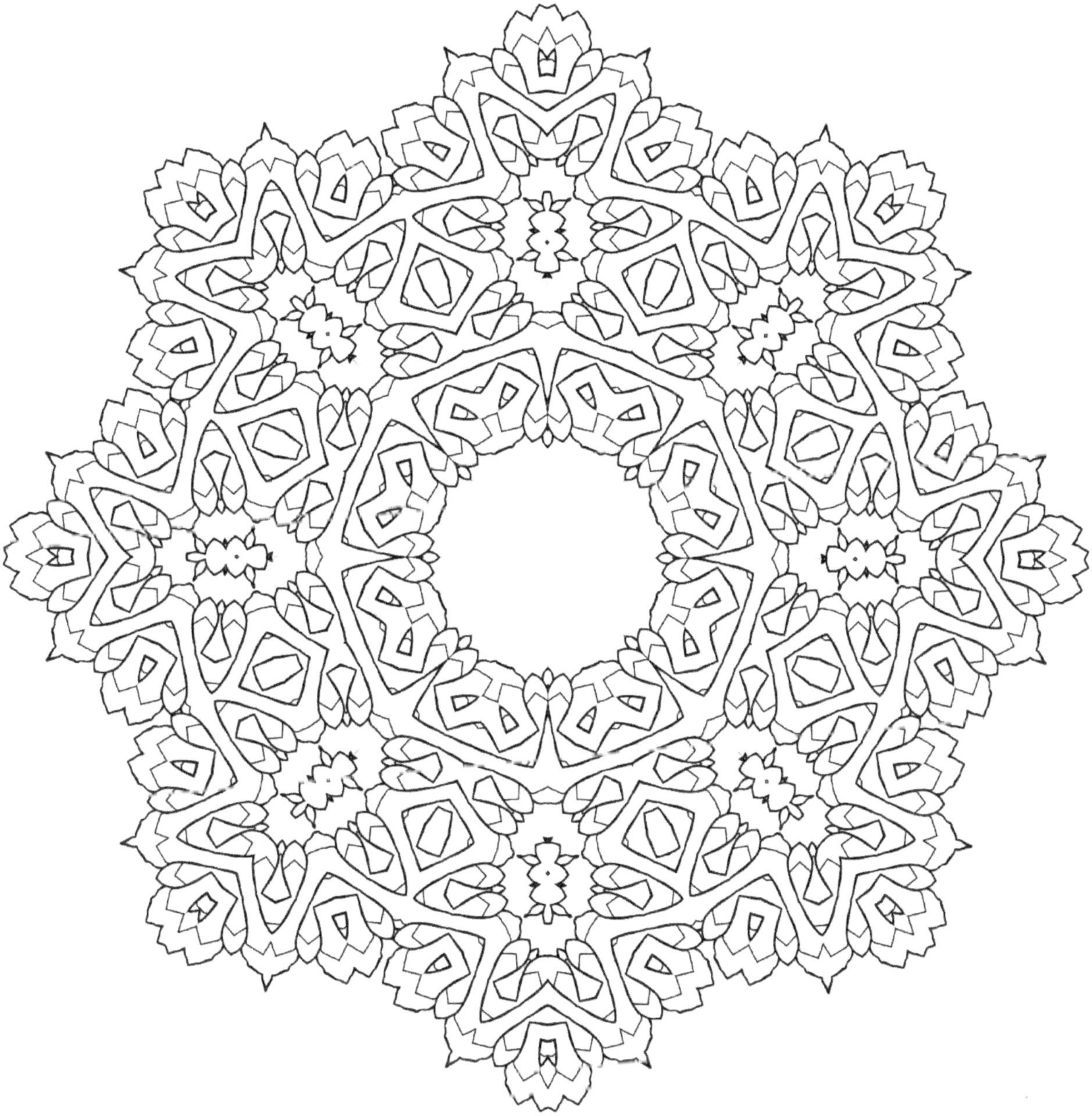

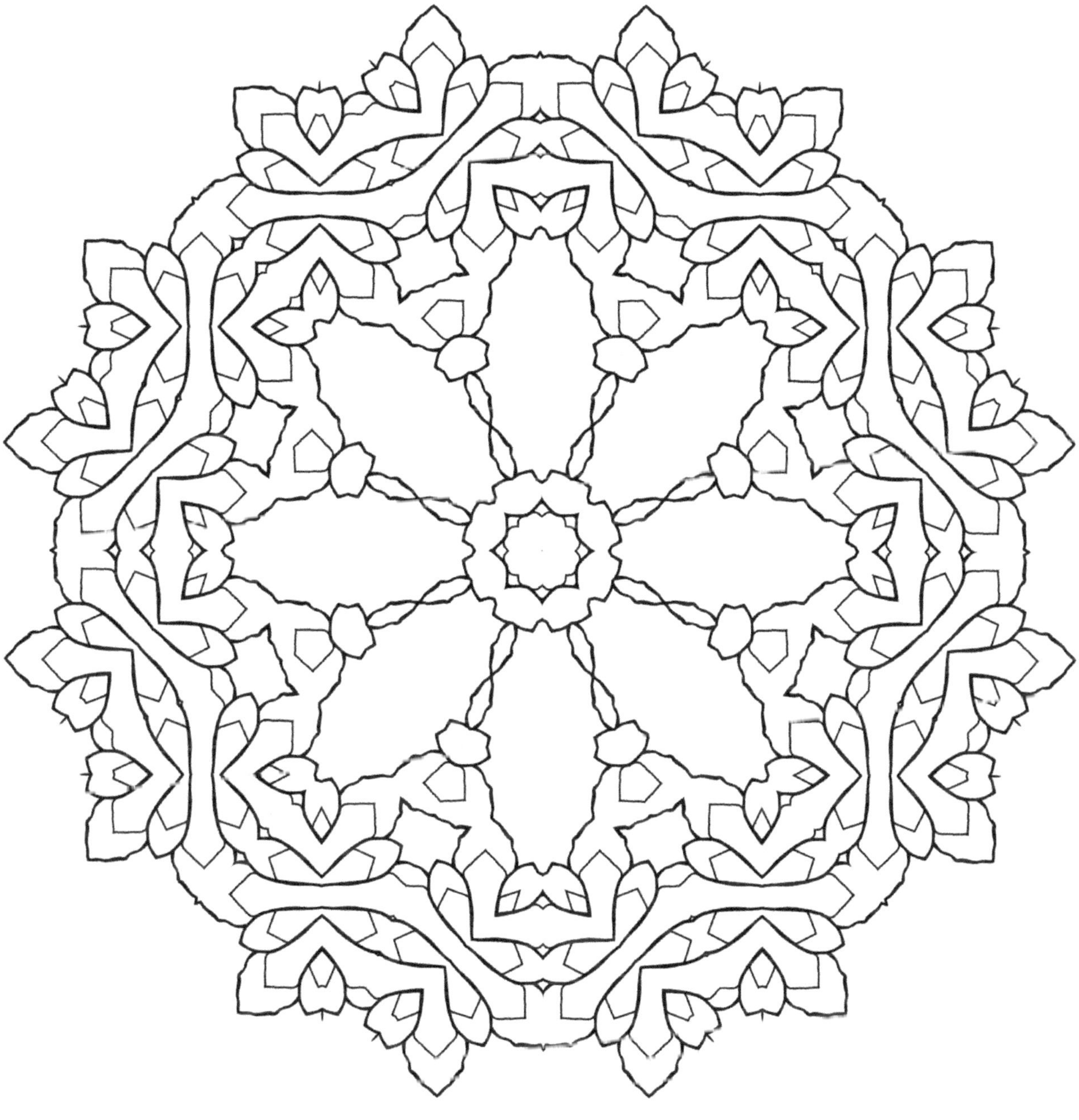

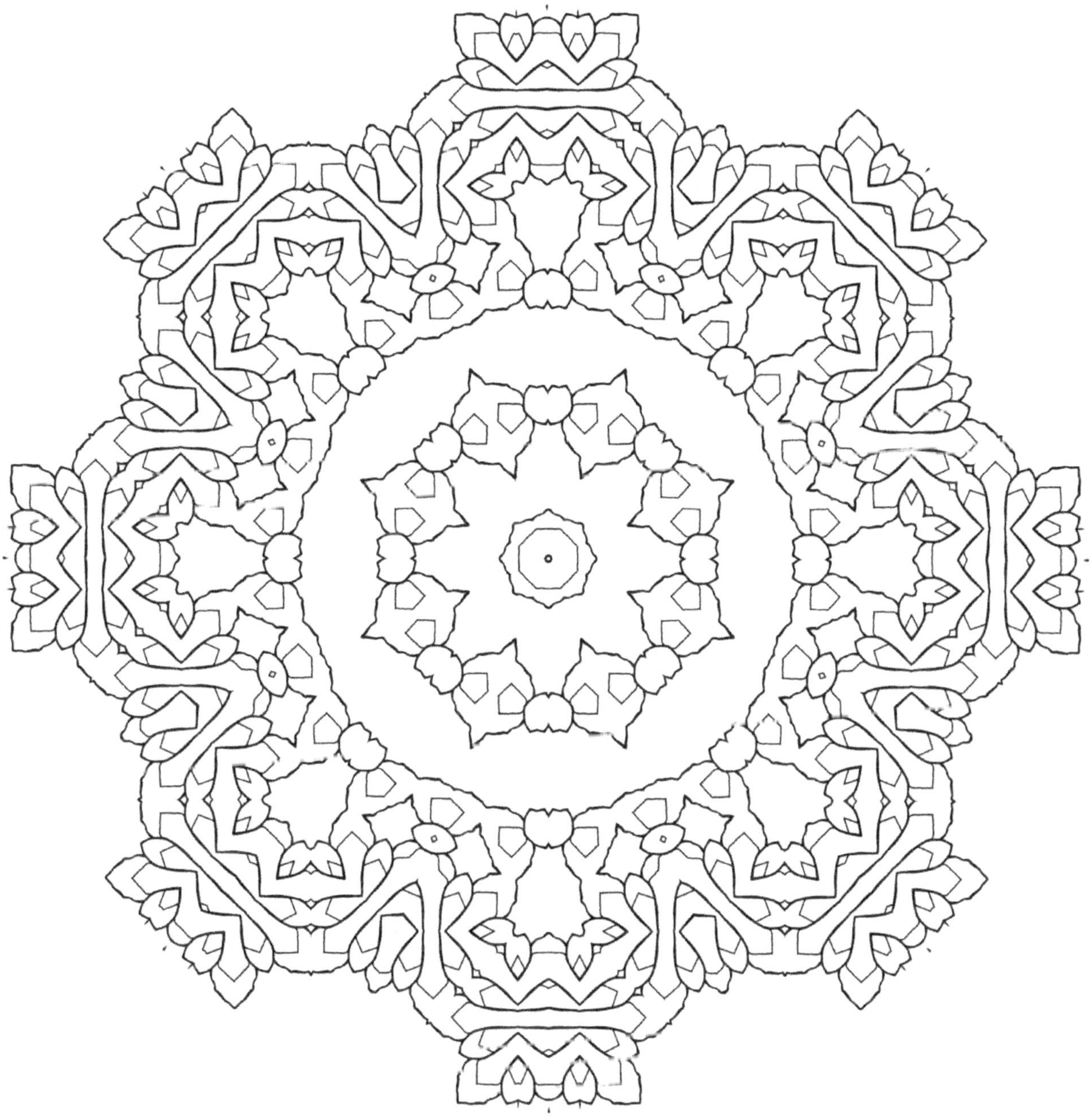

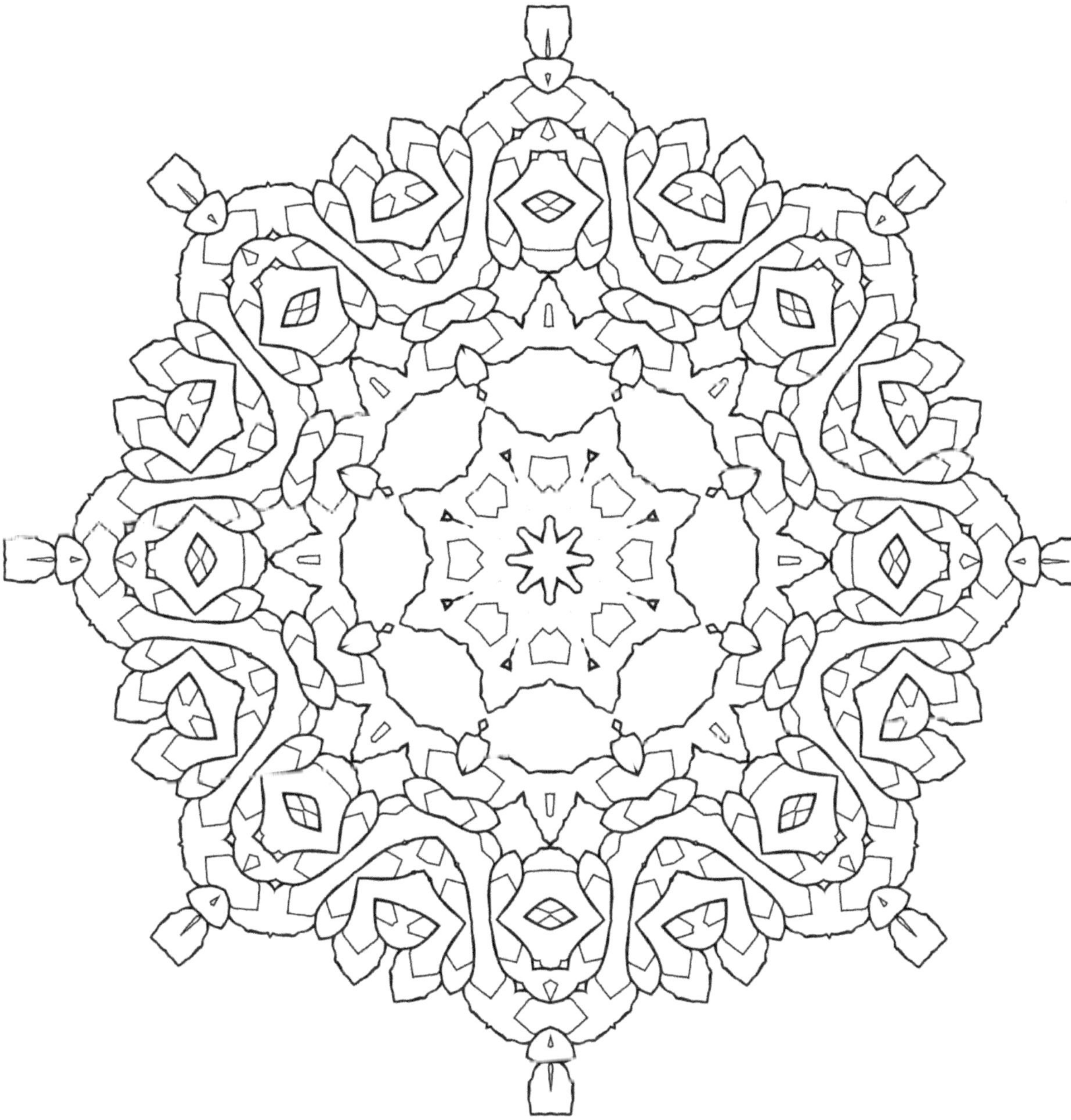

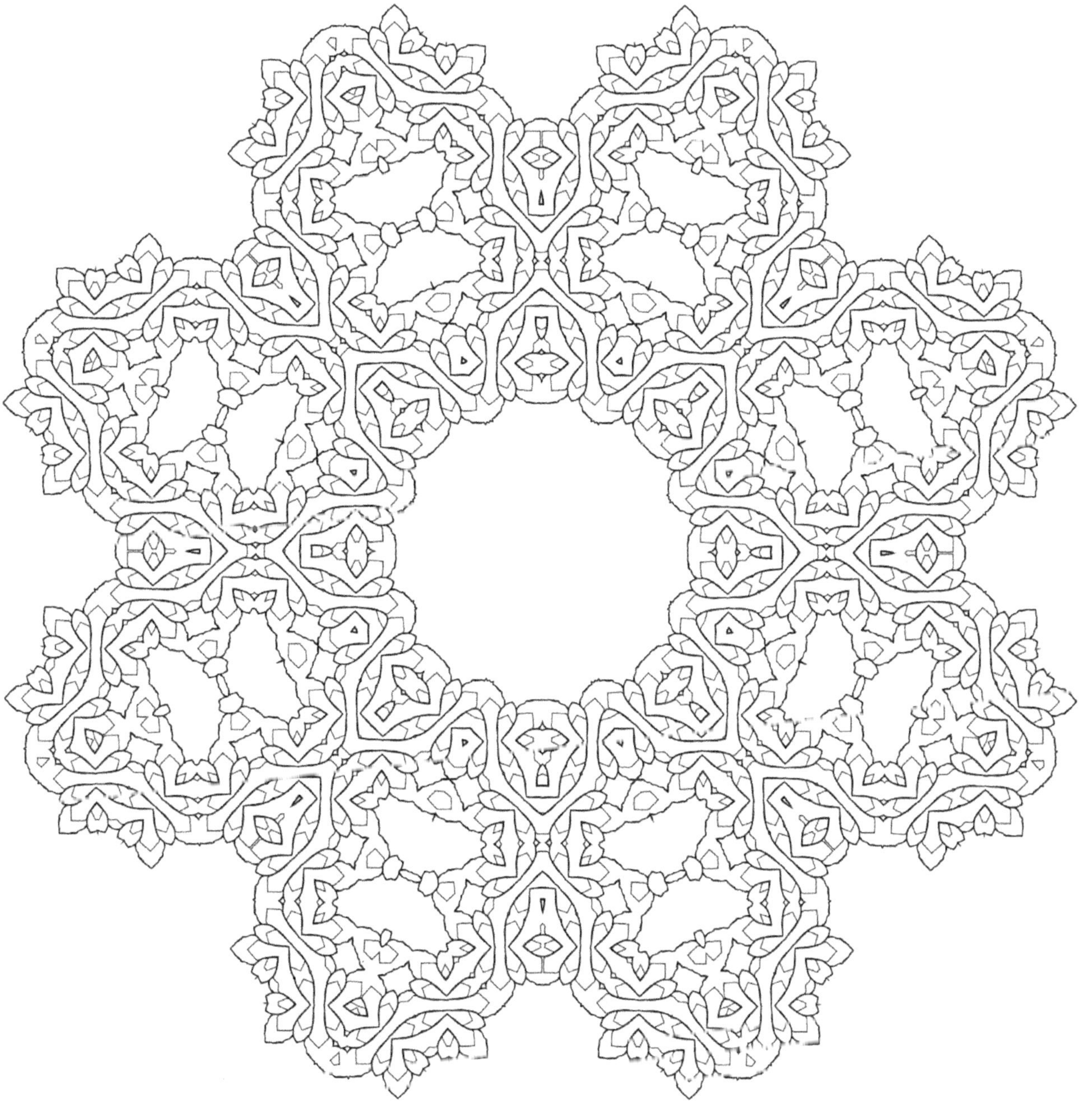

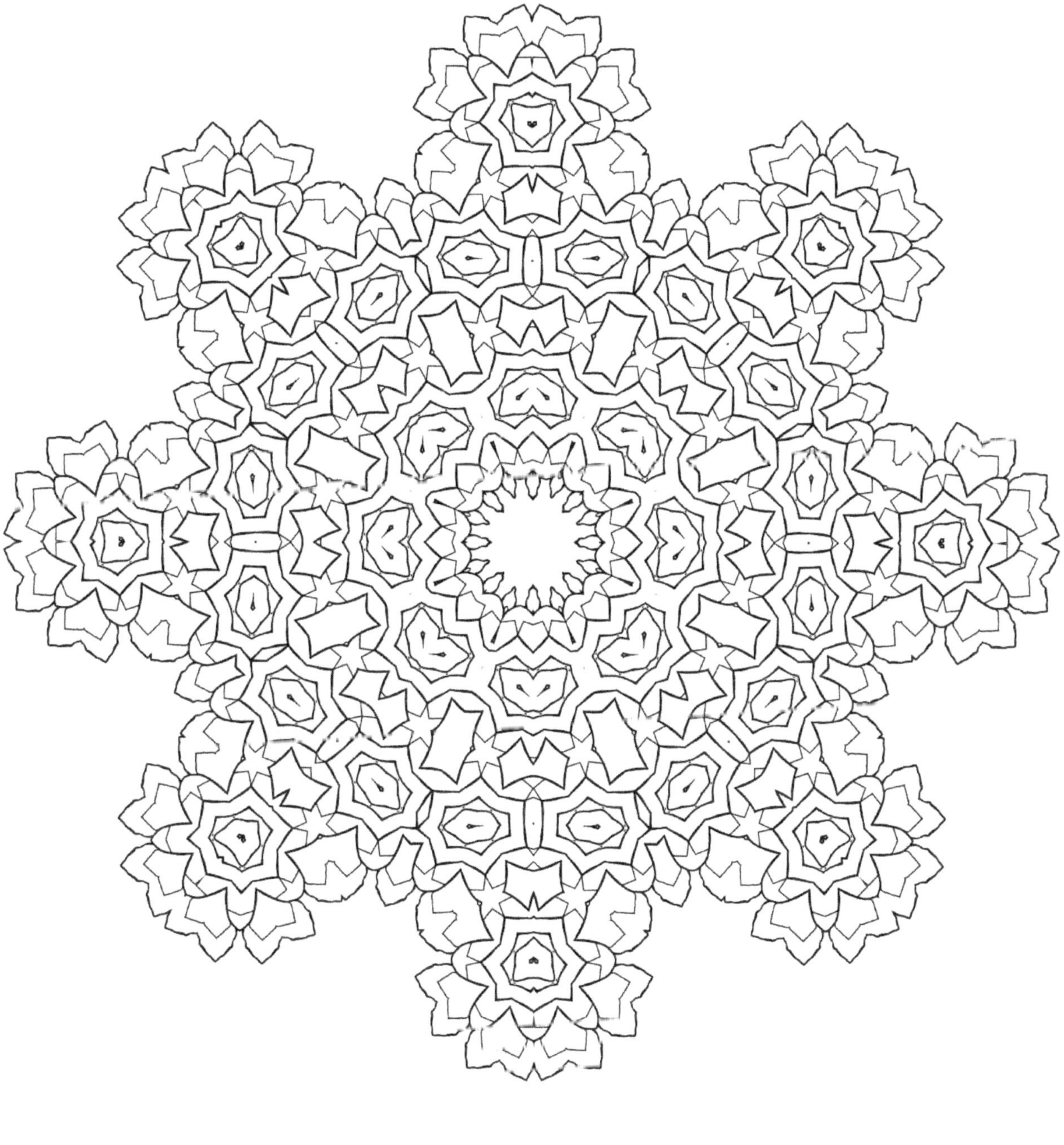

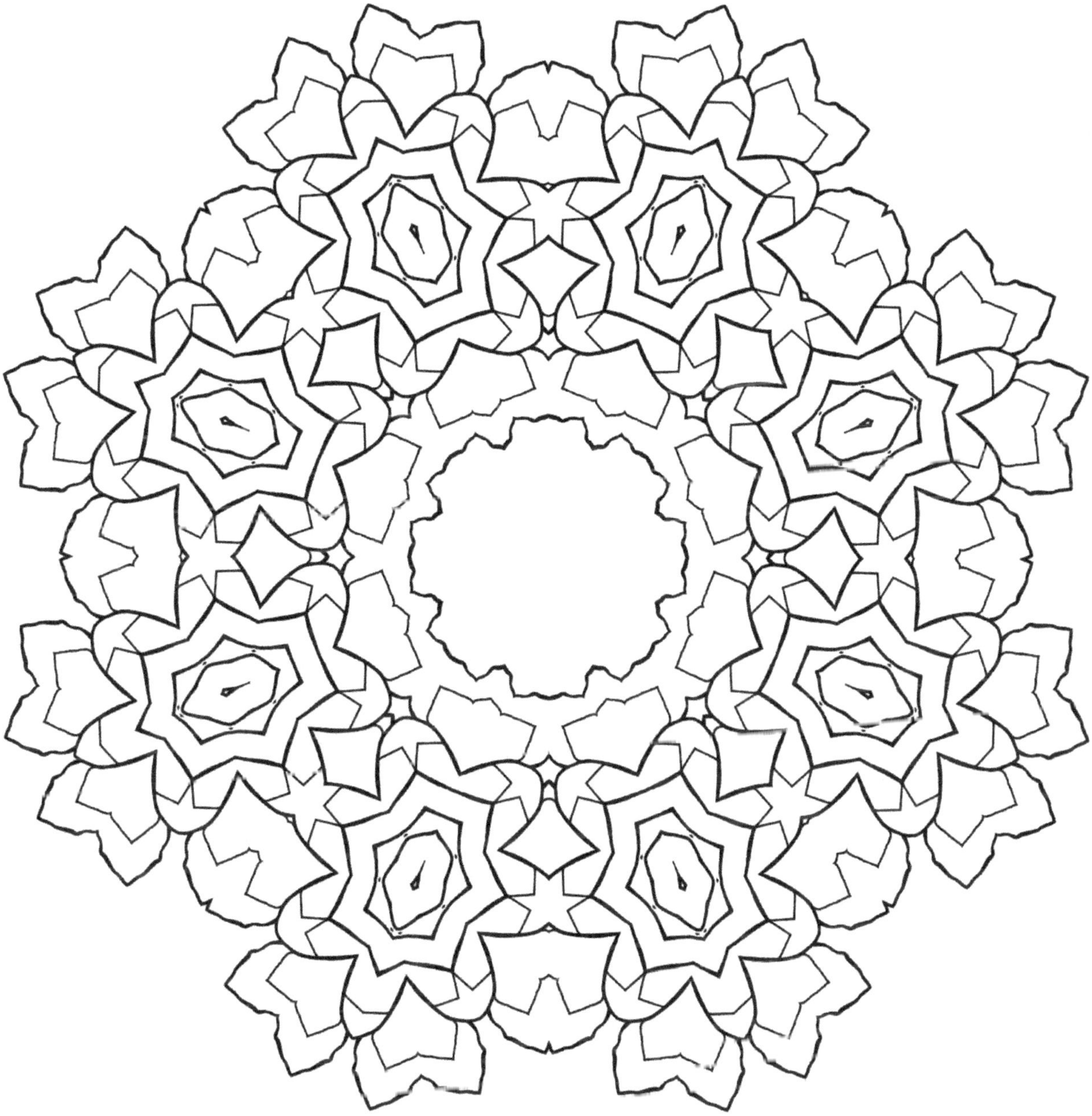

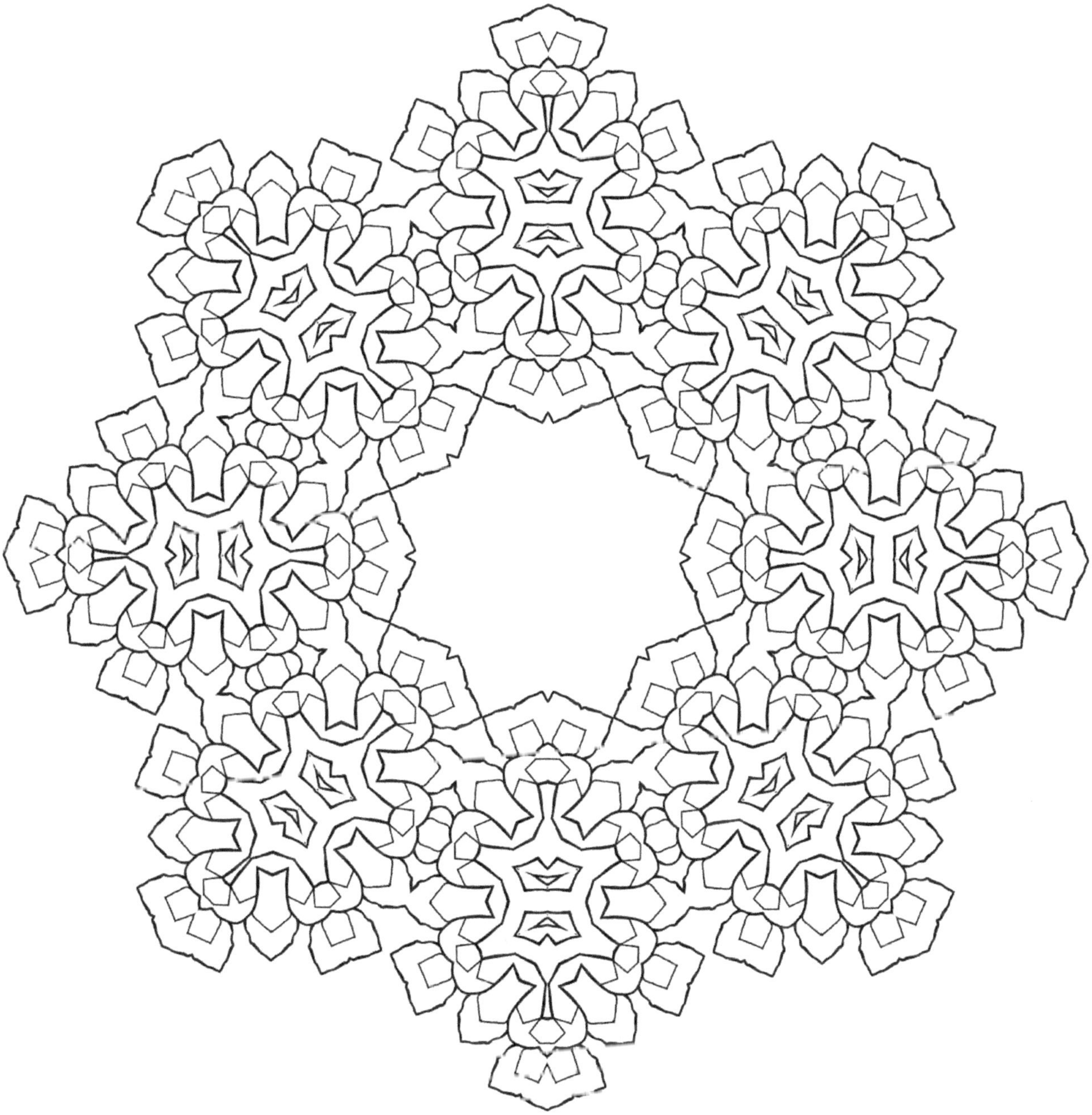

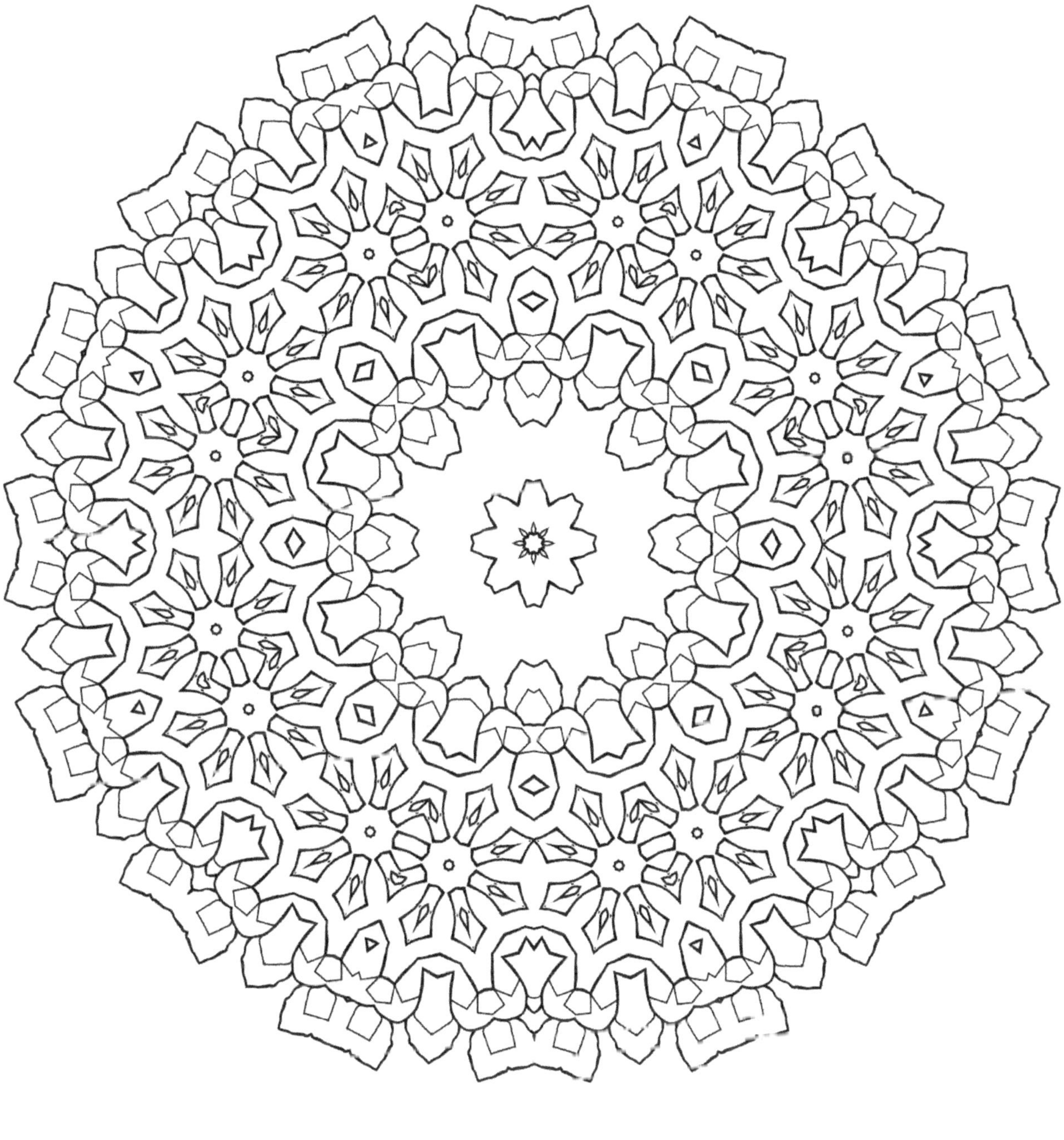

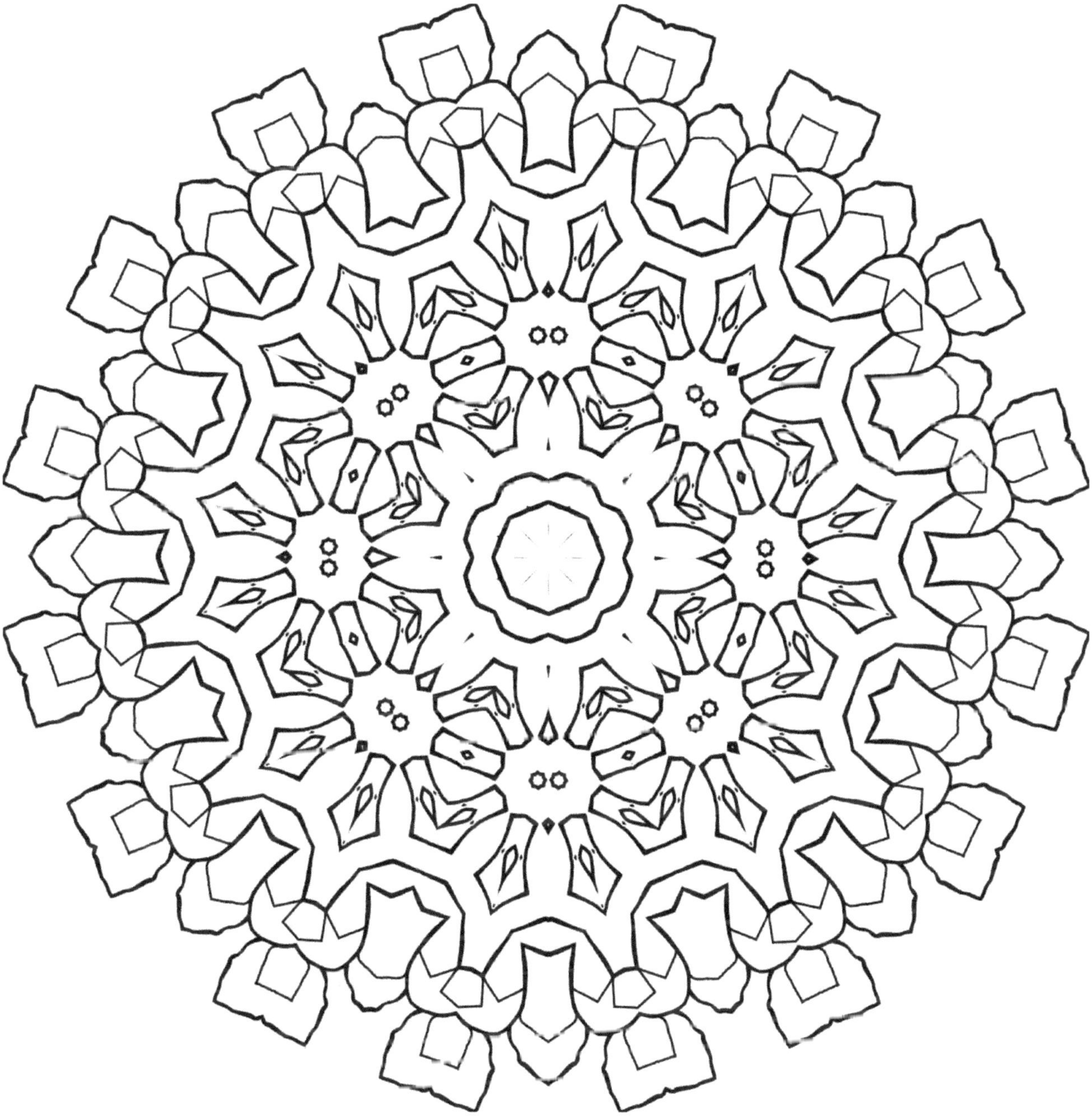

Thank you

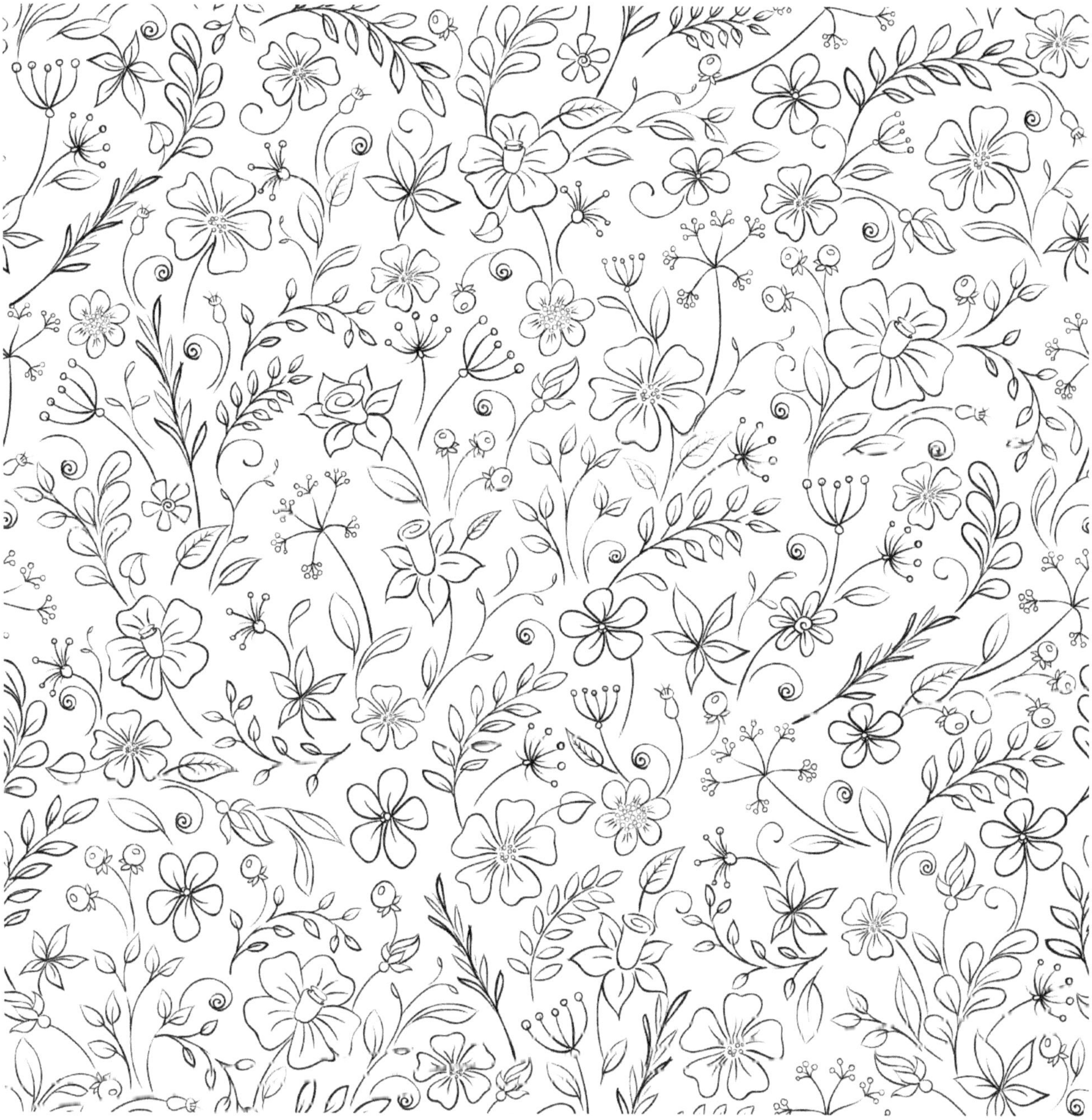

www.ingramcontent.com/pod-product-compliance
Lightning Source LLC
Chambersburg PA
CBHW081115180526
45170CB00008B/2847
* 9 7 8 1 5 4 1 2 9 8 9 0 3 *